This book is dedicated to Montessori educators, teachers, and parents, searching to understand the child and build a better World.

~ Celma Pinho Perry

Living
Creating
Sharing

~

A Montessori Life

By
Celma Pinho Perry

Foreword by
Anna Perry

Parent Child Press
A division of Montessori Services

www.MontessoriServices.com

Celma Perry giving a lecture in 2005

Library of Congress Control Number: 2016900204

ISBN 978-0-939195-46-6

Table of Contents

Foreword v

Introduction: My Story. vii

Timeline of Celma's Life xviii

Lectures and Papers:

1964: The Montessori Directress 1

1964: Montessori's Thinking and Her Educational System 4

1967: The Montessori School of Tomorrow 10

1972: The Challenge: Liberation of the Child 15

1974: The Impact of Birth on Parents 18

1975: Choices 31

1980: Revitalizing the Montessori Apparatus. 34

1981, 1989, 2014: A Montessori All-Day Program. 46

1989: Considerations For Implementing
Montessori Education. 55

Table of Contents, continued

1992: The Montessori Children's House:
Philosophical Dimensions, Practical Implications,
Silence, Wonder, Normalization 58

1997: Reinventing My Professional Life: Montessori and Me 69

2000: The Art of Mentoring:
Passing the Montessori Message to the Next Generation 81

2001: The Importance of Beginnings 87

2001: The Outdoor Environment in Montessori
Writings and Tradition 89

2005: The Great Friendships: Across Continents,
Over Time, Living Montessori 94

2010: Authentic Montessori 101

2011: Authentic Montessori, Chicago Style 117

2012: The Discovery of Silence 126

References. 128

Suggested Reading 132

Acknowledgments 135

Celma and Anna at
a Montessori event in 2005

FOREWORD

It is a pleasure to share this book with the world. A series of papers and lectures, it is the incarnation of a long life of good work, service, and a deep dedication to serving the lives of children and families everywhere. I have always known that my mother was special, different, and that many people actively supported, studied, and followed her work. As both a mother and as a professional partner, she has been my greatest inspiration. Over the years, Celma has also inspired countless Montessori educators, supported the startup of hundreds of schools, and mentored (and hounded) many, many educators to be their best selves in order to better serve our common cause.

If you have never met my mother, you will have to activate your imagination in order to have the right mental soundtrack accompanying your reading of her words. Despite the fact that she has lived in the United States for over fifty years, she continues to have an accent that sounds more like a European lilt than the usual Brazilian-tinged English. We have always attributed this to the fact that she learned English after becoming fluent in French, and her accent in English paid the price. We have worked hard to maintain the cadence and unique word flow of Celma's genuine thoughts and expressions, while smoothing out some of the syntax in order to support broader understanding.

Another resource to hear the passion with which Celma delivers each of her lectures or sessions is the collection of audio recordings that the American Montessori Society has accumulated over the years. Some of Celma's best-loved talks are available for download at http://setonmontessori.org/institute/celmaperry/.

This book has been organized chronologically. Feel free to read the sections in order, feeling the changes and maturations in Celma's perspectives as you go, or skip around to those pieces that call to you in the moment. There are beautiful moments of crisp thinking, philosophical clarity, and many "ahas" that can be found throughout the writings, often in unexpected places.

My heartfelt wish for each reader is that you get to "feel the feel" of Celma's profound understanding, unique perspective, and love of life. She's had a deep preparation, a long career, and her own fascinating personal history, and from this background she opens new perspectives to allow us to better serve our communities.

Anna Perry
Clarendon Hills, Illinois

INTRODUCTION:
My Story

Rio de Janeiro, Brazil, 1948. I was fourteen years old, and one of my high school teachers invited me to attend a seminar in metaphysics that was to be given by a French philosopher. I went out of mere curiosity, and I never left. It became the backbone of my life, a search for what *Is*, a reflection on *Being*. It was to involve a lifetime of study and a continuous sense of wonder about *Life*.

I was born into a military family—my father was an Army doctor—so we moved quite a bit, from the beautiful beaches and mountains of Rio to the simplicity of a small town in the central plains of Brazil. My mother was a professional accountant (something rare at that time) as well as the perfect hostess, always attentive to my everyday needs. I had a house with trees to climb, a small basset hound, friends to play with in the garden, and a working child-sized stove outdoors where we cooked whatever we wanted. The rule was if we cooked it, we had to eat it! My "baba" (nanny) helped us, and since then cooking has been my hobby.

My father loved cars, and every weekend we drove all over Southern Brazil, visiting friends and relatives or just sightseeing. I remember lovely days and nights in little country cottages, on big farms, and in so many beautiful rural areas.

We moved back to Rio when I was six years old; my mother wanted to enroll me at Notre Dame de Sion, Rio's best-known school and the one my cousins also attended. There I learned French. I loved Sion from day one, and my loving kindergarten teacher, Madre Conçeicão, would twenty years later become an assistant in the first Montessori school I directed. I remember thinking at the time, "Someday I will be a Sister, but not a teacher." As my thinking evolved, between age fourteen and eighteen, I built a strong interest in contemplative life. If the highest level of life asks for full awareness of what we are, for full communion with the world, with God, I was going to do it as a contemplative Sister.

Money at that time was scarce. Although my mother's family was wealthy, she and my father divorced when I was fifteen, and that changed things at our house. My little brother was then eight years old and I loved him dearly. But when an invitation, and funding, to go to France to become a novice came from the sisters of Our Lady of Sion, I felt I had to go. With beating heart I told my mother what I wanted, and in March 1952, I left Rio on a transatlantic liner as the leader (albeit the youngest) of a little group of three postulants, on our way to Paris. I didn't know it at the time, but I was heading into what would become the most beautiful and demanding four years of my life.

In 1952

It was in 1954 at "La Solitude," my convent in Grandbourg, a suburb of Paris, that I met Mme. Hélène Lubienska de Lenval, who had worked with Maria Montessori in the 1930s and was then publishing a book, *Le Silence: À l'Ombre*

In 1972

de la Parole, which could be translated as "Silence: In the Shadow of the Word," while directing an outstanding educational program for girls three to sixteen years old. With her, I discovered the Child.

My life took a new turn, from the austere convent—where conversation took place only twice a day for half an hour, entailed intensive manual work making jams for sale, and included many hours of prayer and study—to the daily life of a wonderful Montessori Children's House.

1956 brought me back to Brazil. The learning experience in France, of being a foreigner while staying true to myself, would turn out to be very important for the rest of my life. I accepted no barriers to do what was necessary. Going back to Brazil with a Montessori-Lubienska background, I gained permission to start a Children's House immediately at the Notre Dame de Sion school in São Paulo, a sister school to the one I attended as a child, while concurrently completing my university work. This was exactly the right thing for me to do at that time. Today as I look back, I proudly count all the difficulties that were surmounted—having my religious Superiors, government agencies, and parents accept the program, and then, in a second phase, building the environment and undertaking the constant preparation of new teachers. I admire the strength that was given to me to do this work.

Slowly the Sion school of São Paulo became one of the main centers of "new education" and was known as "Escola Experimental." Our fame spread quickly and in 1961 I was asked to teach a course in pedagogy at the Pontifical Catholic University (PUC) in São Paulo.

A student of Montessori and Lubienska, Father Pierre Faure, S. J., came from France to Brazil to give courses in São Paulo, and I became his assistant and translator. Every summer for seven years, I directed a demonstration class and accompanied Father Faure, becoming more and more sure of my own ideas and presentations through my work with him. I was happy to do the adaptation of three books into one volume from Lubienska de Lenval called *Educacão do Homem Consciente*, loosely translated as "The Education of the Aware Person," published by Flamboyant in 1960, and republished recently in Brazil by Cedet, in Campinas, São Paulo.

Once when I was translating for Pierre Faure I added some personal ideas to his speech and he caught it! "I did not say that," he told me as I apologized. However, he reassured me by saying, "I know now that you are thinking, building your own experiences."

The political difficulties of a country as huge and complicated as Brazil became a daily worry for us educators and university folk. Avidly, we searched for justice, for openness to the poor, for how to share wealth, for how to build a life of human dignity for everyone. I was very involved with the staff of a Catholic paper, *Brasil Urgente*, which called for justice, land sharing, a living wage for farm workers and for the poor. A big political crisis was brewing.

In November 1963, I gave a lecture to the Montessori Teacher Preparation Course I had founded and directed in São Paulo. I told them how education was about dialogue at its core, how we needed to share with each person all that we are, all that we have. Before I knew it, my Mother Superior was visited by a military general who was the father of one of my students (I remember his daughter being so passionate about being an educator). This general denounced my lecture as a Communist appeal, and told my Superior that I must be stopped.

Crisis! What to do? The best idea, if I was to avoid jail, was to leave the country and go to study in Europe. I remember preparing my papers, packing my belongings, crying. I knew I would not come back. What about the Children's House that was now serving children from ages three to ten, and was preparing to start an adolescent program? My student teachers with whom I had worked and guided for so long? I had formed such loving relationships with so many.

Through all this preparation for departure, I knew I would especially miss the thirty-five children whom I had followed as their teacher from the beginning of the first classroom of the Children's House, working and learning with them from 1956 to 1963. These students were the ones who truly trained me as a Montessorian. I remember one day when three of them came to me and said,

> *"The new geography teacher has to go — we can't stand her. She talks a lot and just wants us to listen and to learn it by heart. She gives us no books, no places to research. She knows it all! We can't stand it!"*

I was amazed. The young teacher had come highly recommended, with a bachelor's degree in her area, and had even followed some of my lectures. But as she could not follow the child, could not become a facilitator, we both knew she had to go. Even today this episode has helped me to observe how the teacher relates to the child. I ask myself, "Can she see the child's needs and become a Montessorian?"

Now sixty years have passed since I began with that first group of children and this experience has helped me to see how so many of my adult Montessori students today work on becoming transformed into this approach, some with easy success and others with much effort. I am still in touch with many of these original children who were my first students, who are now beautiful people in their sixties. When I visited them last, they told me they still had a deep friendship among themselves, different than all other relationships they had built in their lives. They meet each year in August to reconnect, and I like to join them whenever I can. We are deeply connected.

Having left Brazil during its political crisis, my new life in Europe brought me to England where I worked with Mrs. Phyllis Wallbank, herself a good friend of Maria Montessori, corresponded with E.M. Standing, who invited me to work in Seattle, and encountered Maria Montessori's son, Mario Montessori, who recommended me for a Dutch government scholarship in Holland. These relationships each helped me to create a vision for what the future could hold.

While in England, just before Easter 1964, I left the congregation of the Sisters of Sion and embarked on my trip to Amsterdam to take advantage of the government scholarship that I was awarded to study the educational system of Holland. I was welcomed as the former director of Sion in São Paulo. The scholarship provided me with a different kind of place and a different kind of job; a limo would pick me up each morning, a guide would ask me which language I preferred, and I had the freedom to study every aspect of the Dutch school system. Leaving church one Sunday morning, I heard a newspaperman announce "Fall of the Brazilian Government, Army takes over, many in prison." A telegram from home told me that the newspaper *Brasil Urgente* had been closed. The final edition, never published, had carried the story of my efforts and hopes as an educator in São Paulo. It had been just over three months since I left Brazil. Many of my friends and colleagues were in prison. A friend, Paulo Freire, who ran outstanding literacy programs for adult workers, went into exile. I was to meet him again in Switzerland in 1972. Other exiles from the Brazilian intelligentsia were welcomed in the United States, at Princeton, Harvard, the University of California, and so on.

During the 1964 AMI (Association Montessori Internationale) Convention in Amsterdam, the theme "Peace" was beautifully developed. I decided there to accept the invitation for a job at Alcuin Montessori, a fledgling school in the suburbs of Chicago. I had also heard of Professor Robert Havighurst in the University of Chicago Department of Education, and applied for my doctorate there. I prepared my heart and was on my way, crossing the Atlantic Ocean again. After days of travel I arrived eagerly in Chicago to meet my new employer. How shocked I was when Dr. Urban Fleege received me in his office at DePaul University with his feet on his desk. These Americans! But his wife Virginia and his three children welcomed me warmly to their house for a few days while I was finding an apartment. I will never forget my biggest "foreigner" mistake. Knowing he knew everything, I asked Dr. Fleege to introduce me to "Mr. Janitor," because this man seemed to own all the apartments listed for rental in the Oak Park newspapers. All the students at the Alcuin Teacher Education program in 1964 heard about my blunder, and we still laugh about it today.

At Alcuin, I was to direct a class of 25 three- to six-year-olds from 8:30 a.m.–1:30 p.m. daily. In the evenings I attended the University of Chicago. As the Teacher Education Program was in session, I was brought to visit one demonstration class and then another. I did not like what I observed, so I decided to go to the library, recognizing that I had come to a place that needed me. The kind secretary told me I needed to observe the third class, directed by Dome Petrutis, the next morning. I hesitantly agreed, unsure of what I would find in yet another classroom. But this turned out to be my first real encounter with Montessori in Chicago; Dome had been trained by Maria Montessori and knew Lubienska de Lenval. What a surprise! I had found my Montessori home and I thanked God for being in America, in Chicago, at Alcuin.

Dome adopted me as her sister; our first social meeting was when she asked me to come home and help her to clean the windows. She knew I enjoyed helping. I met Professor Varnas, Mrs. Varnas, and Maryte Kucinas, a beautiful experience. The Varnases had attended the Montessori course in Nice, France in 1934, the year of my birth. They accepted me into their family. I even learned many words in Lithuanian. Today I am happy to have given many Seton Montessori Institute (formerly MECA-Seton) scholarships to Lithuanian teachers, after the fall of the Communist government. These teachers received their AMS credentials and now have a strong teacher education program in Vilnius, Lithuania's capital.

In August 1964, I also met Hilda Rothschild, a Montessorian who had also been taught by Lubienska and Faure in Europe. Through the years we shared beautiful memories of our unique introduction to Montessori, twenty years apart.

John McDermott, the philosopher of the American Montessori movement, also impressed me as a kindred spirit. Listening to him made me love the United States. Yes, many people here were just like my friends in Brazil and in Europe.

My first American lecture to a group of adult student teachers was a real labor, as my English was not yet fluent. I remember needing the help of Mrs. Kenneth to translate it all from French into English. But during my lecture I put aside the translation and found myself talking spontaneously, adapting my ideas on "What it is to Educate" for the student teachers of Oak Park, IL, like I had done so many other times in France, Canada, and Brazil.

But let me tell you about my first experience at the Alcuin Teacher Education Course. I was asked to direct one of the demonstration classes I had criticized. The student teachers were complaining that the children were not working enough, so the director challenged me to do better. In my youthful confidence I agreed! I had observed the class for three days and noticed four or five children who were very capable. I couldn't sleep the whole night before.

At 8:30 a.m. the next day, I calmly observed as the children arrived, and invited them one by one to work. To Stephen I presented the color tablets, to Peter the blue and red rods, to Marianne the red rods. They became so involved! Slowly the other children all chose a work on their own, and seemingly by a miracle, there they were all concentrating, some repeating an activity over and over, totally engaged. The hours passed so quickly. I acted only as a Montessori facilitator. It was a success!

My life in Alcuin was set. I was invited to be the supervisor of the student teachers and started my life as a consultant. Another experience I will not forget was getting permission to take all the materials and furniture from my class to the gym and spending two days cleaning them, piece by piece, and selecting what I wanted in the prepared environment. Some of the staff considered this scandalous—so much unnecessary work—but some parents arrived to help: the Dunns, the Callahans, the Buckinghams, and others. They knew I had a passion. After fifty years these parents are still among my best friends and I have used these same techniques with my students at Seton Montessori Institute to this day.

1965 was to bring me the joy of building the Montessori Children's House of my dreams as I had planned it long ago in Brazil. As the supervisor of Alcuin's nascent teacher training program, I received two representatives of the Seton Montessori founding Board in my little apartment in Oak Park. After listening to Louise Johnson and Cele Bona sharing their vision and asking for help to find a good Montessorian, I thought to myself, "Instead of finding someone to start the school with them, could I perhaps be the Montessori teacher that they need?" They went back to the group and soon I received my first contract.

Together with Bob Johnson, the founding president of the parent board of directors of Seton (he became an AMS Board member some years later), I designed a Montessori Children's House environment that fascinated me so much that I became an American citizen in 1970. I fell in love with this country through my life in that school and community. I owe that first board of Seton Montessori more than forty years of complete professional joy!

The American Montessori Society had also become a part of my "home." Cleo Monson introduced me to its founder, Nancy Rambusch, who had been trained in England and became a very good friend. I remember her urging me to translate Lubienska's books. I met Doug and Maria Gravel, visited Jack Blessington at Whitby, enjoyed the Donahues, worked with Ginny Varga and Lillian de Vault, Jane Nielsen, Jo Savoye, Jean Miller, and so many others of the Visitation Committee. I have received so much from AMS, and have been happy to share my life within it.

Seton Montessori School continued to progress, with many visitors from across the country and around the world. In 1970 I founded an AMS teacher education program and called it MECA-Seton (it is now called Seton Montessori Institute).

At that time, there were few Montessori teacher education programs in the country. We, the directors of those programs, met each year to share and solidify our American Montessori program directions and guidelines. Today the development of interest in becoming a certified Montessorian brings the number of AMS-affiliated teacher education programs to over one hundred.

1971 marked a new important stage in my life. In that year I decided it was time that I got married; but I had never had a boyfriend! At Loyola University I met a fellow student at a lecture by Dr. Boehlen on "Wonder as the Beginning of Philosophy." Desmond Perry and I became friends, we wondered about the future, and after some visits back and forth to our families, we got married in November

Desmond and Celma Perry, 2008

1972, in Rio. The military dictatorship had mellowed and the country was now moving towards democratization.

We are happy to be celebrating, as of this writing, forty-two years of marriage, and our two daughters, Anna and Cristina, keep us smiling as the years pass. We were amazed when both, after completing their bachelor's degrees, chose to become Montessori educators. Stephen Snyder is my new son. His marriage to Anna in 2001 brought us two grandchildren whom we enjoy and observe as they discover life. Marrying an Irishman gave me a European passport (and a loving Irish family), officially stamping my love for Europe and maintaining our many contacts with the Continent.

With Desmond I have discovered the beauty of companionship. We are together both in our personal and professional lives. Starting on day one he loved the Seton Montessori Children's House that I had nurtured. Together we built MECA-Seton and cultivated the organization. Today, Anna, her husband, Stephen, and Cristina continue the traditions of the Montessori experience that we have worked so hard to build and develop all these years.

On so many of my trips I now make opportunities to meet with my dear friend, Carolina Gomez del Valle. For eight years she lived in Rome at the Central Directorate of the Ursuline Sisters. During this time, Carolina still maintained her heart and her mind in the Montessori work that has made her one of the most admired mentors I ever met. She now travels the world as a Montessori missionary, supporting and leading new communities through the process of becoming inspired by Montessori education. When she was very young, I remember visiting the beautiful Children's House she directed in the outskirts of Mexico City. Carolina's work with the native people there, as well as the finesse, intuition, and love she continues to bring to each human contact, has enriched all our lives. Every time I meet her, on whatever continent, she makes me more aware of my Judeo-Christian roots. I love my roots. I feel comfortable in the Church, even if sometimes I have to fight with some of its decisions and rules.

Years ago I enjoyed preparing the display "Introducing the Cosmos to the Child," geared towards educators of the birth to six age range. It is the fruit of fifty years of work and of experience in the Children's Houses of the world. It was also based on my experiences with countless families, as it starts with the very young baby and the building of his or her own world from day one. Over the years there have been many appearances of the Cosmos Display in the United States, and I have traveled to share it with the growing Montessori movement in Brazil and Slovenia.

Reading Simone de Beauvoir's work on old age makes me so conscious of what is before me for the next years of life. I joyously accept it! I savor the feeling of having been there. I can sit and look without having to "do" any more. Retirement is now a pleasure; I rediscover my philosophical insights, which began as a fourteen-year-old. I see now the importance for me of Being, much more than of Doing.

As I swim every day in the Gulf of Mexico or in the pool, as I walk the sand when my arthritis allows, as I take care of my body and slowly accept its evolution, I become more me, the person I am called to be.

Celma Pinho Perry
Naples, FL
September 2015

TIMELINE OF CELMA'S LIFE

1934   Born in Rio de Janeiro, Brazil

1940–48   Elementary and High School, Colegio Notre Dame de Sion, Petrópolis and Rio de Janeiro

1951   Elementary Teaching Certificate—Escola Normal Carmela Dutra

1952–56   Started as a novice at La Solitude, a contemplative convent in Grandbourg, France with the sisters of Our Lady of Sion. Was introduced to the Montessori/Lubienska orientation course

1956   Internship in Grandbourg, France, at the Montessori-Lubienska Program

1956–63   Assigned to found and direct the Montessori-Lubienska Program from preschool to fifth grade at Our Lady of Sion in São Paulo, Brazil

1957–63   Assistant and translator for Pierre Faure's many teacher education seminars and courses in São Paulo, Brazil

1960–63   Director of the Aperfeiçoamento (Teacher Education) course, which specialized in the Montessori-Lubienska approach, in São Paulo, Brazil

1961   Sabbatical in Paris, France—Institut Catholique

1961–63   Assistant Professor of Pedagogy at Pontificia Universidade Catolica (PUC) in São Paulo, Brazil

1960–62   Diploma in Guidance—Pontificia Universidade Catolica (PUC) in São Paulo, Brazil

1964   London—Studies in English—January–March

1964	Received scholarship (recommended by Mario Montessori) awarded by the Dutch government for study of Holland's educational system
1964	August arrival in New York and Chicago Alcuin School—head teacher of the extended day program, and lecturer / supervisor of the first Alcuin teacher training course
1965	Designer, coordinator, and head teacher of the new Seton Montessori School
1965–66	Lectured for two summer programs teaching Montessori education at the University of Laval in Trois Rivières, Canada
1968–72	Montessori consultant to SPRED, a Catechetical (CCD) special education program
1965–2008	AMS consultant, lecturer, teacher education program director
1970–2007	Founder and director of the MECA-Seton (now Seton Montessori Institute) Teacher Education Program
1972	Married Desmond Perry
1976–2011	Assumed additional role as director of Barrington Montessori School (now Montessori Children's House of North Barrington), a lab school for Seton Montessori Institute
2005	AMS Living Legacy Award recipient
2010	Retired to Naples, FL

☙

THE MONTESSORI DIRECTRESS

An address given to the first Alcuin Montessori Teacher Training Course

Oak Park, IL • August 1964

By Celma Pinho

Do you want a better world?

Do you want a new child?

Prepare a truthful educator.

The preparation of a Montessori directress is very different from any other kind of teacher training. "Directress" is the term that Maria Montessori used to describe the educator, typically a female in her time, to differentiate the role from that of the traditional "teacher." I would like to discuss the sudden transformations and the happy discoveries of life, love, and truth that we witness during the first decisive year in the training of a Montessori teacher.

I have no intention of writing an essay on what a Montessori directress needs to be, but wish to share with you the thoughts I have constantly had in mind since I discovered the Montessori approach and worked as a teacher trainer in Brazil, in France, in Canada, and in the U.S.

The Montessori directress is to be an educator—just this, only this. As an educator she carries within her the spirit (more than the technique) and the technique (always evolving) delegated to her by Maria Montessori.

We have plenty of teachers in our schools, in our homes, in our countries. Do we have enough *educators*?

The educator is the mature human being who is capable of *dialogue*. We could say that we educate in the measure in which we dialogue. To be in dialogue is:

- to be *present*; to be ourselves, very conscious of our own potentialities and limits, *here* and *now*.

- to be *silent;* conscious of the other's presence, listening, open… able enough to give to the others a place in our life, in our thoughts, in us… able to forget our own presence.

- to be *questioning together*… asking and not telling… asking with the other, searching for a better answer, continuously questioning with all our life.

How many people have we met in our lives who are unidentified educators?

The educator is the person who is always listening, always present, always interested in what I am saying, always looking at me, at the reality, and sharing my own discoveries and quietly helping me to grow.

At the foundation of a Montessori training course there must be this very human orientation to help each person to develop and become an educator. This is the very aim we can read between the lines of all Montessori's books. When, for instance, she analyzes the educator as a scientist, she tells us how much we have to be questioning and giving our lives:

And, indeed, what is a scientist? … the type of man who has felt experiment to be a means guiding him to search out deep truth of life, to lift a veil from its fascinating secrets, and who, in this pursuit, has felt arising within him a love for the mysteries of nature, so passionate as to annihilate the thought of himself. The scientist is not the clever manipulator of instruments, he is the worshipper of nature…. it is my belief that the thing which we should cultivate in our teachers is more the spirit than the mechanical skill of the scientist. (Montessori 1967, 4)

Under this light let us see what is necessary to direct the preparation of a new educator, and the different direction we must follow:

1. Discovery of the child or, if you like, "discovery of the true child."

2. Human maturity, complementary guidance in order to be able to be in dialogue.

3. Technical orientation in the different aspects of the "method" and technical training with the apparatus.

Coming to a Montessori training, the future directress has to find a prepared environment in which this truthful "initiation" can take place. In Chicago, Paris, Quebec, or São Paulo, the only criteria to measure the value of a Montessori training are the quality of the environment, the quality of dialogue in depth, the quality of relationships, the possibility and orientation for a conversion for a new understanding of the child, for an extraordinary respect of humankind, of each person and of the child as a person.

Coming to a Montessori training, very often the trainee is looking only for new techniques, for a "new method," for something up to date, just exciting and meaningful. Even though this is probably what she finds at first, we will always remember the student who told us, "I had many courses in psychology and philosophy. Here I was expecting just to learn how to work with the Montessori apparatus and, instead, found the child as a person, like me, eager to be himself."

❧

Montessori's Thinking and Her Educational System

An address given to the first Alcuin Montessori Teacher Training Course

Oak Park, IL • October 1964

By Celma Pinho

When a person has had an experience of love and of truth, all her life is changed, beyond the visible frontier—over herself, over humanity, over God. At the base of any school renovation exists someone so immersed: the educator.

What was this tremendous experience that influenced Maria Montessori to become an educator and to bring to us an educational system that has endured more than 50 years?

I would like to stress an excerpt from a lecture given by Montessori in London on May 6, 1929. She expresses an idea that you will find repeatedly in all of her books:

We treat the child as if he has no mind, because we do not know that [the] child needs an action that can put him in contact with the reality, so that he has a strong perception of his own dignity. No one has more right than the child to satisfy his innermost needs, because the child is constructing the man of tomorrow.

These needs, when they are not satisfied, reflect in the adult that the child is going to be, as a block in his mental development, as a deviation of the character, as psychic anomalies that make the personality weak and unstable. The child that did not learn how to do for himself, how to perform [on] his own, how to give direction to his will, will become a weak adult who cannot live without support.

As all philosophical study of an educational system involves the analysis of the concept of man (the aim of all education is the whole human), I would like to give you another very simple thought of Dr. Montessori's, and an assertion made by many Montessorians and constructivist educators who believe that movement is necessary to integrate within learning experiences. I think that this is more than a psychological principle, it is a fundamental philosophical attitude about humankind, that the person is both mind and body:

The child learns through movement.

Learning = action of the spirit, of the mind

Movement = action of the body

We are going to analyze today the strong, experienced perception Maria Montessori had about the child as a human person.

It was from her perception that her educational technique was born. Montessori contributed more to education than all philosophers have. This is her revolution. She made a school for "man," for this person that is the child. In the history of philosophy we see that St. Thomas Aquinas's magnificent analysis of humankind, learning, and teaching (in his work *De Magistro*, "On the Teacher") had indeed no influence in the educational systems. Aquinas believed in the connection between the mind, soul, and body. The educational systems continued to be influenced by the Platonic dualism (the soul and the body as separate entities), and we now see this reflected in traditional education: e.g., in order to think, the body must be still. Montessori brought to education her deep perception about human nature, about the child's nature. The environment is prepared for the child to touch and experiment in order to think and understand reality.

***

We are going to consider:

- Montessori's philosophy of humankind
- Montessori's psychological study of the child

To accomplish our first aim we must answer the question:

What is a human being?

If we analyze the little excerpt of the Maria Montessori lecture, we see she believed that "man" (a human) must:

- Be put in contact with reality to have insights and satisfy his inner-most needs
- Do for himself/perform his own actions; he learns through movement

In other words,

I. The human has a unified body and mind

II. That she/he has a mind (spirit) means: she/he has an intelligence she/he has a will

Intelligence

What does it mean for a person to have intelligence?

The human intelligence acts through the body.

To understand this reality, we can quickly do an analysis of knowledge:

Looking at, touching, or smelling an apple, I can know apples, I can name "apple," I can have a universal idea about apples.

Without my senses, I can't have a universal idea about apples.

"Nothing is in the intellect that did not come first through the senses." (Thomas Aquinas, *De Magistro*)

Knowing intellectually what an apple is means to know from one apple the general idea of "apple" which is transferable to all apples in the world. Man cannot know anything without a previous experience that comes from the senses, that comes from immediate contact with the material reality through the senses.

You see now the philosophical idea that is within Montessori materials. This is why we always have contact with the concrete reality before we learn a concept. For example, in order to help the child have the idea of number (e.g., one, two, three) you give him the red rods, the blue and red rods, etc., because you know how the human spirit works.

Maria Montessori had this philosophical idea of human intelligence and human knowledge present in her mind when she prepared the environment for the child.

Traditional schools are always forgetting this. It is why what the teacher says is more important than the student's experience. This is why traditional schools develop the child's memory more than they do an attitude of interest in discovering.

Will

Analyzing the Montessori environment, you will understand the Montessori idea of human will. Maria Montessori had great respect for the great power of the child's will. That is why she emphasized respect for the child's work rather than interfering with the work of the child. She believed that a human strength is the ability to choose for himself, to determine for himself the best way, seeking the Good.

Maria Montessori did not believe in training the child. As Montessori teachers we must remember that the child has an intelligence, that the child has a will.

The human is a substantial unity of a body and a mind.

In the Montessori approach we always have a person before us who is a body animated by a spirit. All the movements of the child must be willed by him—this is self-control, this is, in a sense, normalization—to do with his body what he wants.

But, as we have an order of values, we must know, principally, that the human is a spirit in a body (for example, all knowledge comes by the senses, all love is expressed by actions.)

While the traditional system in schools separates the body from the spirit, the realistic Montessori pedagogy respects human nature. How?

In the Montessori classes the child thinks through moving and moves through thinking. In traditional schools they believe the child must be absolutely quiet and immobile on a bench in order to think.

***

I hope this very simple analysis about the human person can give you an idea of Montessori's philosophy. For Montessori, the child is not a person in miniature, but a person in construction.

From these insights you can analyze why she is so respectful of the child, and why we must all be respectful of the child.

THE MONTESSORI SCHOOL
OF TOMORROW

An address given to the second Alcuin Montessori Teacher Training Course

Oak Park, IL • September 1967

by Celma Pinho

The Montessori movement today is still "yesterday." Too many Montessorians are "yesterday people," repeating without rethinking what they are doing. Maria Montessori was not "fixed," but *we* tend to be more "fixed" than necessary. She was constantly innovating, constantly asking, trying to discover how to help the child. As directresses, we should also keep asking, researching, continually improving, and updating. We should read more in the psychology of education and child development. (Read Nancy Rambusch's 1962 book *Learning How to Learn*.) Are we doing enough research? Dr. Thomas Banta has done some, and Dr. Ann Lucas of Fairleigh Dickinson University has studied the relationship between the ideas of Piaget and Montessori. But are Montessori schools doing as much as they can to incorporate the results of new studies?

We are pretty sure of the general goals of Montessori promoting the child's growth—independence, freedom, discovery, experience, and so on—and we have a method and materials. What more do we need? Do we "spell out" our methods sufficiently, so that we can separate and get at the different aspects of the general goal? This is what we do when we study the curriculum of our preschools.

Jerome S. Bruner, in *The Process of Education*, puts it in these words (1977, 69):

> *In planning a curriculum, one properly distinguishes between the long-run objective one hopes to achieve and certain short-run stops that got one toward that objective. Those of a practical turn of mind are likely to say that little is served by stating long-term objectives unless one can propose short-run methods for their achievement. More idealistic critics may too readily dismiss short-run educational goals on the grounds that they cannot see where they lead. We are inclined to take a middle ground. While one benefits from clarity about the ends of education, it is often true that we may discover or rediscover now ultimate objectives in the process of trying to reach more modest goals.*

Perhaps Montessorians need to think more about the "short-run goals." How can we do this? We are indebted to R. C. Orem for the following statement about the preschool curriculum (which he credits to a 1965 Head Start publication):

> *Curriculum for teachers of four- and five-year-olds is harder to pin down in words than for elementary school teachers, where subjects, such as arithmetic or spelling, are understood. For preprimary children, curriculum is harder to describe and really quite different to teach from academic matter. You teach everything you know and are, and everything children want to know about and are becoming, and you teach it in little children's terms.* (Orem 1967, 89)

What do *you* understand about "curriculum?" (In the ensuing discussion, the following were among the definitions that the group put forward:

- Curriculum is a plan of action directing the total environment to encompass the child's experience for the development of the individual child and his needs.

- Curriculum is a general, organized outline of procedures for educational aims and, secondarily, a step-by-step process in presenting these aims, including academic subjects.)

Traditionally, curriculum has been thought of as a plan of studies that helps the teacher to organize and direct his own work, as well as that of his students. All subjects, each one organized and all structured together, make up the curriculum. According to current thinking, *curriculum is the total addition of the students' experiences planned by the school as an institution, taking into account teachers and students, methods of teaching and of work, materials and environmental atmosphere.*

How Do We Plan a Curriculum?

1. First, there is the long-term goal, the long-run plan for the whole school, based on a precise conception of man and the universe. It takes into account, among other things, (a) social and cultural factors, (b) the child's social experiences, and (c) needs of the community. We sometimes fail to consider the social and cultural factors; the school *must* be responsive to the background of the child, which affects his experiences, his sensory acuity, his motor development. Maria Montessori saw the teacher as a communicator, a programmer, and an exemplar. She is a bridge, the preparer of the environment, the one who provides the short-run steps to fulfill the long-term objective.

2. The curriculum must be planned by the ones (*all* the ones) who are in charge of the education of children: *all* teachers in a school; teacher *and* assistant in a class; the administrator and the Board.

The unity of the school depends on the unification of the main goal. Then it comes down to short-run steps: each teacher will have her own goals for her class; each area of development (e.g., geography) will have its short-run, as well as long-run, goals.

3. It is the educator's task to create an atmosphere in which the curriculum can be developed. Do I realize my responsibility for this, for planning the curriculum? To educate is to help man become conscious of reality—his own reality, the reality of others. Consciousness leads to responsibility. This is our long-run objective.

New developments in curriculum planning for elementary and secondary schools, as discussed in Bruner's *The Process of Education*, are also relevant to a discussion of preschool curricula, for at this level, too, one cannot be indifferent to the concern for the "quality and intellectual aims of education" and to the ideal of education as a "means of training well-balanced citizens for a democracy." (Bruner 1977, 1)

Bruner sees the problem of planning a curriculum as the problem of how to teach the underlying idea, the basic structure, of whatever the child is learning about and how to teach it in terms the child can understand, whatever his age or ability. He advocates teaching a fundamental structure and then providing learning conditions that foster it.

Compare those ideas with the Montessori concept of the prepared environment. Bruner urges that current curricula be reexamined, because they "often lose their original form and suffer a relapse into a certain shapelessness" (1977, 54). Examples of reexamined preschool curricula may be found in *Pre-School Education Today* (1966, edited by Fred M. Hechinger).

The Necessity of Evaluating

If you set goals, you need to stop and evaluate them.

1. The teacher's evaluation

2. Assessment at the preschool level

Conclusion

The concept of curriculum for the Montessori school of tomorrow can be summed up by this statement: *all in the school must serve education.* This requires analysis of the school organization in which each staff member and each aspect of the environment must be oriented to the personal development of each child.

❧

THE CHALLENGE: LIBERATION OF THE CHILD

Outline for an address at the American Montessori Society National Conference

Chicago, IL • Spring 1972

by Celma Pinho

I. The Situation

Walking through Chicago, Mexico City, or Paris, or visiting with families in Geneva, Milan, or Rio de Janeiro, the perceptive observer of what is offered to the young child by our industrialized society discovers violence and oppression.

Born of father and mother, the child is expected to live according to the rules of their world:

- A world where he is often not welcomed (do not touch, do not move); an adult-sized world where he is uncomfortable.

- A world where he must, in order to survive, accept the rules of the group at the expense of his own becoming.

An analysis of the child's reality is necessary:

- Who is the child? Who is this child here, now?

- What does he need for becoming the person he is called to be?

II. The Impact: A Need for Revolution

"The greatest difficulty in the way of an attempt to give freedom to the child and to bring its powers to light… lies in overcoming the prejudices which the adult has formed in this regard." — Maria Montessori (1949/1989, 44–50)

The aspects of this revolution:

- Conscientization (or "critical consciousness," a concept developed by Paulo Freire): invite the child to become himself

- Awareness and responsibility: believe in the child

- Dialogue and creativity: be yourself before the child

- Characteristics of a free world for the child

The challenge: liberation of the child

- Analyzing the child-adult relationships at any level, in any given situation (home, community, school), one would be struck by the fundamentally disrespectful ("I know all—you know nothing"), moralistic (this is the right way to do it), and narrative (adult tells, child listens) approach that is used by the adult.

- Aware of the child's potential, those committed to liberation must discover for the here and now of each life the proper techniques to educate man, this conscious being who is always relating to the world around him.

We do not have pre-fabricated methods. The characteristics of a free world for children must be taught by the community around them. In rural areas or in industrialized cities, in Africa or North America, let's awaken in the adults a desire to become truthful educators who are able to build, not with bricks but with their attitudes:

- An environment that frees
- An educator who is in dialogue with the child

III. The Challenge

1. Creating new environments able to free the child

   a. At home

   b. In the community

   c. At school

2. Training adults as educators

   a. The parents

   b. The community

   c. Early childhood professionals

THE IMPACT OF BIRTH ON PARENTS

An address at the American Montessori Society National Conference

Boston, MA • June 1974

By Desmond and Celma Perry

"The fact that will always keep and bring us all closer together is the nakedness and helplessness of the newborn human child…. Once the newborn is here and is to survive at all, there must be a certain well-delineated environment of care adapted to the stages of human growth."

Erik Erikson, *Dimensions of a New Identity* (1974, 81–82)

On the broad plain bordering the Adriatic, just north of the town that was then called Ariminum, an insignificant stream threads its way through the marshes to the sea. In 69 B.C. it marked the border of Cisalpine Gaul and the Roman Republic ruled by Pompeii and the Senate. One winter day in that year, Gaius Julius Caesar came with his legions, fresh from the conquests in Gaul and Britain, crossed the stream, and thus began his overthrow of the Republic and his eventual rise to dictator. The river was called the Rubicon and ever since it has symbolized a transition, a crossing over from one state of life to something very different.

Celma and I believe that we crossed our particular Rubicon when we learned that Celma was pregnant. While we crossed the street to recover our wits in the nearest coffee shop, we were mentally executing huge evolutionary leaps of consciousness-raising. What would it mean? Should we change houses? Go to California? Stop smoking? The only toast I could think of for Celma as I raised my glass was, "May your shadow increase!"

On the face of it, Celma and I had little to be concerned about. We had both wanted to become parents. We both had given many lectures to parents and had just recently returned from giving a series of courses to parents of preschool children in Brazil and Panama. Theoretically, we knew a lot about early childhood and how to educate children. We were both Montessorians and had read *The Absorbent Mind* (1963), *The Secret of Childhood* (1936/1981), and *The Child In The Family* (1956). But we couldn't help recalling that at the end of every course we had given in Latin America, someone would always remark, "I wonder what you'll say in a few years when you are parents yourselves." The Latin peoples are so delightfully realistic!

Now, up against reality, we couldn't help being apprehensive and fearful. Did we really know how to cope with this new life that was still only a tiny embryo, less than 1 inch long? Would our professional life, hitherto so satisfactory and enjoyable, be upset? Where would we find models to follow in preparing for this birth and the education from birth of our child?

The Conventional Wisdom Of An Adult-Centered Society

We were not much impressed with the patterns of child-rearing accepted in our society. We felt critical of practices like:

- Exposing children to television from an early age, even sometimes using television as a babysitter.

- Leaving children with babysitters night after night so that they do not build a stable relationship with their parents. The quality of care given to such children is often poor and they respond by becoming fretful and whining.

- Regarding children as a bother and a nuisance, and therefore excluding them from most aspects of adult life, like family meals, social occasions, and churchgoing.

- Bottle-feeding babies because breastfeeding is more trouble.

- Not allowing babies to move around because they break things and need constant attention; and keeping them in cribs and playpens. Perhaps as a result of this, many babies feel cold and have to be wrapped up in too many clothes or kept in overheated houses.

- Letting children become more immersed in the world of Disney cartoons and comic books than in the real world.

- Caring exclusively for children's physical health, while they become nervous, irritable, and perpetually overexcited.

It can be fairly said, I think, that our society is not a child-oriented society. Children are regarded as a bother, and an expense. Zero population growth is regarded as an ideal; "none is fun" is the slogan of many young couples.

The way in which we design our houses and our furniture reveals this attitude more clearly. Infant beds are high, so that the mother need not stoop. Playrooms or family rooms are in basements so that the adults need not be disturbed. Modern apartments envisage families with two or fewer children. Door handles and bathroom appliances are high; power sockets are low.

Getting Ready

Celma and I both had had the experiences of working with children in Europe, in North and South America, and, in my case, in Africa. (One of the advantages of marrying later in life is that one has a fantastic amount of experience to draw upon.) We reread Montessori and found out all we could about the Lamaze method of natural childbirth and the ideals of the La Leche League. We tried to incorporate what we had experienced into what we were learning and to work out some basic principles.

To begin with, we started by analyzing the importance of a happy, healthy pregnancy for the development of the fetus. We were aware of Freud's still-controversial teaching that the mother's psychological well-being during pregnancy affects the future well-being of the child. So we eased up our schedules, let our social life slide a little, and tried, in a relaxed way, to be happy people. At the same time we both adopted a physical regime of light exercise, simple food, and no smoking or drinking. Celma's doctor advised her to use no medication whatever, not even aspirin or allergy pills.

At first we tended to think of our child as a teenager and to pick out where he or she would go to college. The Lamaze course we attended in Celma's last months of pregnancy helped bring us closer to earth and it helped crystallize our thinking in three areas of immediate interest:

1. What does a very young child need?

2. What impact would a baby have on our own personal and professional lives?

3. How could we prepare a growth-filled environment?

    a. Personal environment: *we* (the parents) are the place where children live and grow

    b. Our house, especially the child's room, toys, etc.

I would like to take these points in order, to share what we decided to do, and how our decisions worked out in practice.

1. The needs of a young child

One of the amazing things about Montessori is that modern research is "discovering" so many things that she pointed out over a half century ago. She talked often about the shock of birth and how we should protect the newborn child from bright lights and loud noises, and keep his environment as simple and as natural as possible with a minimum of clothes, an environment that permits movement and is stimulating to the senses while being safe and orderly, an environment that will lead the child to develop all his powers through activity so that he can soon master himself and increase the life space where he exercises mastery.

Modern medical science still lags behind her thinking, but it is slowly reaching her level of understanding. We chose a pediatrician, Dr. Paul Dunn, who thinks about Montessori as we do, and was a founding member of the board of Alcuin Montessori School in Oak Park, IL, as well as of the American Montessori Society.

Abraham Maslow, in *Toward A Psychology of Being* (1962, 25), speaks about the basic human needs, which must be fulfilled if any human being is to grow in a healthy way.

Ladder of Basic Human Needs

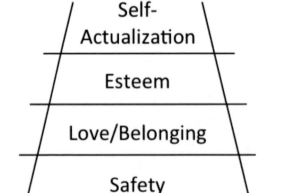

The second most basic need, once physiological needs (food, sleep, etc.) are met, is for safety or security, and this need is fulfilled for the very young child very simply by holding him, by holding him lovingly and often. The next most basic need is a sense of belongingness, the sense that he belongs in this family, who live in this house, and who accept him unconditionally as one of their own. When he feels physically and emotionally secure, accepted in a particular family group, he needs the experience of being loved for himself. For the small child this sense needs constant reinforcement, by holding, touching, glances, gentle words, forgiveness, and reassurances. Only when he feels sure that he is loved and therefore is lovable can he go out of himself and become a loving person.

Incidentally, Montessori, in *The Child In The Family*, calls parents the Love-Teachers, who build on the child's natural love of the adults on whom he depends. She writes beautifully of the child who, early in the morning, goes to wake up his insensitive parents who are not aware of his needs during either their sleeping or waking hours. Her point is that we must be open and responsive when the child begins to show his love for us.

Maslow also speaks of the person's need for status, a sense that we have a respected place in the scheme of things, that we have certain rights and duties, and that these rights cannot be arbitrarily changed or taken away, even at the wish of a loved parent.

We took note of what Erikson said about the small child building up his unconscious sense of basic trust during the first year of life. He learns from the trustworthiness of his parents that people are to be trusted, that life can be trusted, and that he himself is good and can trust himself. We read Piaget and especially what he said about human development in the first years—the sensory-motor period.

Sensory-motor stimulation in the first year:

Tactile:

Floor: rug, wood, tile

Clothes: choice of fabrics, size

Toys: texture and shape

Visual:

The human face

The mirror

Dim lights, natural light

Toys: colors and shapes

Auditory:

The human voice

The music box

The total environment: soft, natural

Thus far, we were still in the realm of theory, but as the birth approached, hard decisions were to be made.

2. What would be the impact of the baby on our lives?

The first decision was to be with our child as much as possible during the first year. Our apartment was about an hour from the school, and was on the twenty-first floor. With some regrets, we left the lakeshore and moved closer to the school into a townhouse with plenty of grassy open space around it. We chose a hospital that had a family-centered program, which means that the child stays with its mother throughout the day, and the father can remain all day with them. We would have preferred having the child born at home, but Celma's doctor vetoed this idea because she would need hospital care; in fact, she had to have a Caesarean section.

We decided on breastfeeding if possible. This made life more complex because of the time it took and it required keeping the baby near its mother for feeding times. We made sure that the hospital staff had a positive attitude towards breastfeeding. For her first three months, Anna had no other food except breast milk. She was very healthy, free of colic and respiratory infections, and increased in weight and strength like any normal child. She was happy to be breastfed until eight months. Our experience of the happiness and security it gave both to our child and to Celma leads us to feel very strongly that every child has a right to be breastfed. We decided that our child must be treated as a person from the start, as a full member of the family. So she would be entitled to as much comfort, consideration, and time as any other person in our home.

Stemming from this, we decided that, as parents, we would need to try consciously to be happy. This baby was going to revolutionize our lives, to give them new directions. For her sake, we needed to be open to these changes and create a sense of happiness when we were with her. We love restaurants, and Anna soon got used to quiet corners in the local pizza parlors. Even when she filled her diapers three times during one meal, we learned to laugh and to cope gracefully. Anna also discovered the acoustic qualities of churches and took a delight in screaming there, usually at the most sacred moments. Now she knows the church grounds about as well as she knows the inside of the church!

Celma and I love traveling. Our families live in Rio and in Dublin, and Anna has traveled without difficulty to meet her relatives in both places. We enjoy our work. We direct a preschool and a Montessori training program. Celma gives many lectures here and abroad. Anna soon got used to listening to Celma's lectures and she liked having a second bed in the school office when both of us had to be at school together. We rearranged our schedules so that one of us could be at home with Anna most of the time.

We decided to build the mother-child and father-child relationship in a conscious way. This required pursuing activities suitable for the child. Swimming lessons are a delightful experience; so is walking in the woods, or spending time on the floor exploring all the possibilities of movement—rolling over, sitting up, crawling, pushing and pulling objects. We took the television out of the living room and keep it in our bedroom. We use it only for the evening news and a very occasional movie. Now the emphasis is on activities we can pursue together as a family. We feel that in this way all of us can grow together. Family meals and family play are shared features of each day.

3. How to prepare a growth-filled environment, the personal environment?

As I have already indicated, we prepared for the birth of our baby by freeing ourselves from commuting long distances and by changing our lifestyle so that we could spend more time together as a family. For times when we both have to work, we knew that Anna would be cared for by someone who is a friend of ours, a grandmother, and most important of all, a very loving person. Anna generally goes to Grandma Seraponas' house and now she looks forward to these outings as enjoyable variations in her routine. Since Anna's real grandmothers live so far away, a surrogate grandmother, who lives nearby in Clarendon Hills, is a necessity.

While Celma and I want to share with our child our Brazilian and Irish backgrounds, we realize that she is an American. Celma speaks Portuguese to Anna so that she will feel as ease with her Brazilian relatives. I speak English to her so she can acquire a proper brogue for the folks in Ireland. Both of us set about becoming more familiar with American history and folkways, so that Anna will feel at home in this culture. While there is no shortage of critics of America, we believe that every young person in America should somehow experience first the lonely heroism of the first explorers, the idealism of the founders of the Republic, the glory and tragedy of the Civil War, and that he should be proud of his country before he can have the right to be critical of its less attractive aspects.

Anna's Physical Environment

This is probably the subject that occupied most of our thoughts during the pregnancy. We prepared a room for Anna in our new quarters that was simple, cheerful, and easily kept clean. We kept in mind some principles during our planning:

1. Research shows that young children are interested mostly in human faces, or lacking real faces, in pictures of human faces.

2. Color schemes affect mood, and careful choices here can promote a calm, peaceful outlook.

3. Natural materials and fabrics are preferable to manmade fabrics or plastics.

4. Furniture should be child-sized, able to be opened or manipulated even by a one-year-old.

5. The environment should be beautiful and artistic.

6. It should be orderly, with a place for everything.

7. It should invite movement and activity during the child's waking hours.

We found vinyl wallpaper with really artistic drawings of a boy and a girl to cover two walls, a low wall mirror, and a teak sideboard that we converted into a cupboard with the help of a small drawer unit. We floored the room with wood tile and a large soft rug to cover the area near the bed.

We bought a large basketwork patio chair, suspended on a strong metal frame, for a cradle. We took down the basket, and set it horizontally suspended from above by two strong wires. This served very well for Anna's first three months and we kept it near our own bed. When she was three months old, we got an extendable teak bed from a Scandinavian store. It was very low and we made it lower by cutting off the legs about four inches above the floor. She could then roll or crawl out of bed without danger since we padded the rug near her bed with two fluffy pillows. A few times when she was restless at night we placed a small board by the bed to prevent her rolling out by accident, but she quickly adapted to the new situation and only got out of bed when she chose to. We left some toys on the rug and she often got out of bed, played with her toys and dropped off to sleep on the rug. When we put her in bed, we needed to get right down to the floor and kneel or sit beside the bed. We always tried to stay with her long enough to get her settled down for the night.

We chose clothes and bed coverings that allowed for movement and that displayed a variety of textures and colors to stimulate the senses of touch and sight.

We followed the same principles in choosing toys for Anna—variety of color and texture, stimulation of the senses, encouragement of activity and exploration, and had no more than two or three toys to choose from at any one time. Hanging toys helped her begin grasping at around three months, but then she became more interested in the boxes the toys came in than in the toys themselves. We also allowed Anna to experiment widely with different foods and new tastes. One thing we find is that, if presented properly and patiently, any food can be appreciated and enjoyed by a young child.

In general, then, our experience with Anna reinforced our research. It convinced us of the need for a human environment that is warm and gentle, an overall environment that is natural and reasonably stimulating, one that permits the child to move and to work at his own growth. So, away with cribs! Give the child a low bed and a warm rug in his room. Away with playpens! Make the house safe for a baby and be ready to teach him how to crawl up and down stairs. Don't fill his body with chemicals or drugs, and don't drug his mind with television until he is ready to take it in his stride.

What Montessori Offers

We feel that Montessori gives parents a few basic tools that can help them in their task:

1. **An attitude of respect.** When we realize that the child is a person with all the rights of a person, we may have to stop emphasizing, "This is MY child" and begin to allow him to develop his own independence, his self-discipline, and his responsibility for himself. So we can give the lead to the child in courtesy and self-respect, and then allow him to be with us, to eat with us, and to work with us.

2. **Techniques for creating an environment that is natural and stimulating.** The environment must be child-sized, orderly, and consistent, allowing for experimentation and adventure, constantly readapted to the child's physical and intellectual needs as he grows. It should stress materials and foods that are natural, and should include the possibility of playing with water, sand, and mud, and of getting gloriously dirty at times.

3. **Techniques for intellectual development.** The ability to give a three-period lesson is a great help. The little child will learn whatever is well presented to him. His intellectual development comes from his sensory-motor contact with reality. His ability to name reality comes slowly and we, as parents and educators, can help him to understand reality as he finds the words for it.

So let's say we want to teach a child the names for two colors.

First Period: the adult points to a red tablet and says, "This is red." Then he points to a blue tablet and says, "This is blue."

Second Period: the adult says, "Show me blue." "Show me red." The child shows them correctly. If not, repeat the first period.

Third Period: Verify if names were assimilated. Everything now comes from the child. Typical question: "What is this?" The child will respond, "This is red." "This is blue."

4. **Techniques for scientific observation.**

These include:

   a. Total presence and attention

   b. Silence: allowing the facts to "talk" to me without
      interruption

   c. Questioning attitude: an observer has no ready-made
      answers

   d. Give it time: collect many facts, in different situations,
      and analyze and test them before drawing conclusions.

What do I observe?

1. Observe the child as a totality, the child as a result of a particular
heredity, a particular past, and a particular environment.

2. Observe each area of his personality.

   a. Physical development: Be aware of what is regarded
      as normal. Be aware of what are the child's needs at
      each stage.

   b. Emotional development: The studies of Maslow
      and Erikson are very helpful here.

   c. Intellectual development: Be aware of Piaget's genetic
      epistemology. This awareness helps us to realize how
      the child is progressing cognitively.

Many forces in our adult-centered society are proving hostile to the family in its task of child-rearing. Maria Montessori's genius was to discover and unleash the potential locked up within the child. Our task today is to stand back and give the child enough freedom to build himself within a planned environment.

☙

CHOICES

An address to a Parent Meeting at Seton Montessori School

Clarendon Hills, IL • October 1975

By Celma Pinho Perry

As a child is to be born, we all gather, wondering who she/he will look like.

How right we are! Our children will bring in their bodies, in their lives, the marks of our families—the marks of our lives.

When does a child's life start?

We could say that the beginning of a child happens long before conception. Each one of us carries the results of many generations. The genetic and social heritage is there. We cannot choose our own, but we will depend on its imprint.

Being from the south of Brazil, all of my family has dark eyes. My children have blue eyes! Blue eyes being recessive, I spent time studying my genealogical roots. In fact my great-grandparents came from Holland; my mother gave me the genes that, combined with my very Irish husband's, created the blue eyes. Our children are the result of generations of choices. We will continue to share these choices with our children. Wouldn't it be wonderful if we could, from early childhood, awake within each child a respect and love for life?!

Our choices, our habits, and our daily lives combine to form the body that will hold the being of our child. It is before conception that we need to moderate drinking or quit smoking or develop healthy habits since our body carries all the imprints of our lives and our children will be the result of these imprints. We all know cases of children born without a limb because we didn't know the effects of thalidomide in the 1950s. I will never forget the night spent with a good friend after the birth of his child. The child had no arms or legs, just a trunk, the result of the mother having taken drugs. I have many choices before I conceive, before pregnancy, or before birth. In fact, I can choose my "world." What do I want to pass on to my child?

Defining my world is difficult. Most of the time we live from one event to the next without reflecting. As a baby is to be born, let's identify our values. Let's become aware of our goals, let's purify our interests. The first thing I will give to any newborn child is my world, the world in which I live.

I will never forget my experience visiting the little apartment of one of my colleagues in Paris. A happy Chinese man, he received us with a lovely Chinese meal on plastic plates and cups. At the end of the table his little baby, eight months old, ate from a gorgeous Chinese dish. He told us, "I kept the beautiful dishes for kids, because I want him to have a Chinese soul."

It's not only the relationship with our partner and pregnancy that gives us a child. It is the world in which we receive the child that first mothers him. In the same manner, an adopted child becomes my child by the immersion into the daily living that my world provides.

As a child is to be born, parents have a chance of choosing—choosing again the same life path they have been living, choosing again the world they have known, or discovering again who they are and celebrating who they are. A new birth in the family is a moment for new choices, new awareness of who we really are, of who we really want to be for the child. A new birth is a moment for joy.

When a woman is pregnant she needs to be very gentle, very kind to herself. Whatever happens to her is happening to the child within her. What she eats, what she enjoys, her troubles and fears too. A pregnant woman must be very careful with herself. Before birth she is the environment in which her child lives. It is important to create an environment where the people around her are also aware of this growing child.

Pregnancy and parenthood are good times for reflection. The child comes into our world to learn from us the *art of living*. Desmond Perry, in his book *The Child Is a Person* (1974), describes how painters in the old times would go to live with a master to learn the art of painting. Today we have pictures and, because they are so similar, we do not know if they were painted by the master or by one of his disciples.

Having spent all his formative years as a part of the master's household, the apprentice would be presumed to know enough of the craft to take his place in society as a responsible adult. Apprentices would flock to a highly skilled craftsman and, in later years, would boast about the fame of their old master.

Our children come to our lives as *apprentices in the art of living*, the art of being human. Our *choice* of raising a child calls us to refine our perception of our own lives, as we know our environment is where they learn the art of being.

Revitalizing the Montessori Apparatus

An address at the AMS National Conference, Consultants Group

New York, NY • June 1980

By Celma Pinho Perry

I. Introduction

I must begin with my own educational roots, the very moment when I chose to be a Montessorian, to address the American Montessori Society Consultants. The full challenge of our work is to constantly deepen our answer to the same question that nagged Maria as well as all educators from all cultures over all the centuries.

What does education mean? How are we to educate? I owe many of my thoughts to two teachers who influenced my career, Hélène Lubienska de Lenval and Pierre Faure.

Lubienska patiently and passionately studied education. She shared her brilliant insights with me as I sorted through my choices. I promised myself that I would continue the tradition she started with the same commitment that she had, and

- remain open to the astounding revelations of observation;
- be aware of the scientific world and its contributions;
- be devoted to continuous change and adaptation.

In choosing to be a Montessorian, I did not

- abdicate my right to think;
- receive an educational system that was closed; or
- receive a treasure that must be hidden and preserved just as it is.

The first eight years of my life as an educator focused on assimilation of what Maria had discovered, as passed to me through the insights of Madame Lubienska and also Madame Bernard in Paris. Lubienska's main book, *L'Education de l'Homme Conscient* (1953), which I adapted to Brazilian culture in 1958, was, and still is, the base of my educational philosophy. Through Lubienska I was repeatedly immersed in the main points of the Montessori philosophy and of Maria's techniques.

Slowly I discovered that to truly be an educator I had to become aware of Reality:

- My own Reality
- The Reality of the world around me
- The Reality of all people, especially of children

I also devoted much of my time during those early Montessori years recreating, with fidelity, all I had seen in the Montessori classes of France.

The second period of my introduction to education included reading the work of Jean Piaget, A. S. Neill, and John Dewey. I listened to and read about many others who were being discussed at the time in the corridors of the universities and along the world's highways and byways.

It took time for me to understand *how* Maria had worked; how much she had studied, thought, and listened. I gradually understood that I had to follow her steps in order to continue and advance her work, not merely repeat it. The impact of this discovery made me, I hope, an educator—as Maria was.

As I address this group of consultants today, I would like to discuss with you how AMS can *continue and advance the discoveries* of Montessori.

Perhaps a better title for today's session would be *Teaching Children How to Think*—as this is the role of all the apparatus (Piaget and Inhelder, 1969).

II. The Children's House

I remember the first supervision I received in the United States from a consultant for the Illinois Department of Children and Family Services (DCFS) in one of the first years at Seton Montessori School.

First, she told me for half an hour that she did not agree with Montessori and she was coming to see if we could update some points. A little disappointed and lost, I just invited her to sit and observe my little people. For two hours she actively followed all the happenings. I had no way of knowing what she was thinking. I felt good about my work and was happy to discuss it with her. Finally we sat down after the children left, and she asked very seriously: "Is this a Montessori class or a 'Celma's class'?" The question made me think. Yes, this was a "Celma's class," based on the Montessori insights and my updating them for our children in this community, based on my own background. We passed our visit with enormous success.

From this day on, I knew I could open my doors to any consultant. I was ready for dialogue. This class was not merely a Montessori class; it was my class, and I was a good educator.

As consultants, we visit so many Children's Houses. How could we describe an acceptable Children's House for today's world?

A good Montessori class is *not* just…

- a class that has all the Montessori materials;
- a class in which everything is color-coded, new, and shiny from left to right and bottom to top;
- a class where all ground rules are respected;
- a class where everything is very quiet and everybody obeys.

What is a good Children's House?

A good Montessori class could best be described in terms of *relationships*. It is primarily a *well-prepared environment* directed by *an aware educator*.

My main preoccupation today as a teacher educator is:

1. To share with my student teachers the *core of the Montessori philosophy*.

2. To introduce them to *the labor of observation* and have them relate to children as Maria did.

3. To awaken in them a *thirst for more and better understanding of the child* and of the apparatus, through studying, reading, analyzing, visiting… any means at their disposal.

III. The Montessori Apparatus: Teaching Children How to Think

Our aim in building up an environment for children is not primarily to give skills and information. Our aim is, through the offering of many options of activity, to create a place where the children can actualize all their potentials.

In Montessori we are concerned *with process*, not with product.

For example: How do I add? What is this mental operation more than the fact that $2 + 2 = 4$ precisely? We want to teach *how* to think more than *what* to think. How do children think? How could I, as an educator, be with children so that they become more and more aware of reality?

Trying to advance Maria Montessori's discoveries today, I have to concentrate my efforts in studying the work of Jean Piaget and its implications. I will focus on the relationship of the thinking child to the environment (Piaget, 1969).

The development of intelligence is a continuous process of construction from birth to adolescence *in a sequence that is the same for all children in all cultures.* I have learned that knowledge is constructed by the mental activity of the person. The way in which knowledge is acquired is not merely through the senses — from outside sources — but *through action upon the environment and through interaction with the environment.* In fact, we interact with the environment through our cognitive structure, which transforms the sensory information that we receive from our environment (Piaget, 1969).

Our aim as educators is to enable the child to develop his total cognitive framework. In the structuring of knowledge, the child will evolve from purely behavior schemes into what Piaget (1969) describes as:

1. Physical knowledge

2. Logical mathematical knowledge

3. Representative knowledge

The transformation begins in infancy, and comes to correspond more and more closely to reality as the cognitive structures become richer and more elaborated. The child goes through many stages of constructing the structures. The sequence of this development is the same for all children (Piaget, 1969).

Our task as educators is to help children elaborate their knowledge with a rich and coherent framework so that they will learn all through their lives and adapt well, not only to what already exists in the environment, but also to a world that we cannot even imagine. We must help them develop the ideas that they will construct with their cognitive and affective structures.

Piaget showed us that four factors affect the intellectual development: maturation, experiences with physical objects, social interactions, and equilibration. No set of apparatuses can ever tell us how to teach (Piaget, 1969).

The Montessori prepared environment creates a place where, as Carl Rogers says, the child discovers "I enjoy the discovery of order in experience" and also realizes, as Rogers expresses "Here I feel I can be myself" (1961, 24). A stimulating organization of her world provokes the child to think.

Maria Montessori did not devote her time to preparing environments, but to converting adults into educators.

The Montessori prepared environment

Knowledge is acquired by a process of *construction* rather than by *absorption and accumulation of information* from the external world (Montessori, 1963). Are we as Montessorians sure of this? How do we present activities? How do we present key concepts?

When I show something to a child, he receives it at the level in which he is living and not at the level that I am giving.

We must put the accent on observing the child so we know what the child is learning rather than what we think we are *teaching*.

We must put the emphasis on listening to the child's spontaneous representations rather than expecting the right answers. We must be where the child is and, as Montessori did, *we have to follow the child*.

When the child has well-elaborated cognitive structures, he can arrive at the correct answer to a variety of questions as an obvious logical necessity.

The Montessori approach, in this sense, absolutely conforms with Piaget's studies. The other approach we often see in classrooms is to try to teach every skill, rule, and piece of information, in the hope that something will be remembered and transferred to other situations. I am sure, as Montessorians, we cannot fall into this trap.

It is really important to *treat skills as tools* in the service of intelligent living and not as the source of intelligence or goals in themselves.

The Montessori apparatus exists for the child — to *provoke children to think.*

We know well that we are not to teach by being the only source of feedback. This would be education by conformity to the person in authority. On the contrary, children have to be taught to develop confidence in their own ability to figure things out. If children make an error, it is usually because they are using their intelligence and reasoning in their own way. Every error is a reflection of the child's thinking. The teacher's task, as Piaget said, is not to correct the answer, but to figure out why the child made the error (Piaget 1969).

Let's remember again, *teach teaching, not correcting.*

But can we ever *teach* children? What can we teach? In what areas does the child construct his own concepts? How can we encourage children to think? Let's remember Socrates who continuously talked to students by questioning them. When they asked him, "Why do you constantly question us?" he told them, "I am only the midwife to your thoughts."

In visiting Children's Houses I have encountered teachers who think:

1. "I am a Montessorian when I work with the apparatus."

I still remember this fantastic class I visited during a hot summer day; the children were outside raking, swimming, planting, watering plants, talking, and walking, and the teacher told me, "Excuse me, Celma, today my children are not doing Montessori." I stopped and asked myself, "What the hell are they doing?" What they were doing was gorgeous. It is a common concept to think that we teach as Montessori only when we work with the apparatus. I call it a static fixated attitude.

2. "I want to be a good educator, but my children do not respond to these materials, so I need to go out and learn the best of every theory

that exists and bring everything to my classroom." This temptation is called eclecticism.

My personal experience as a Montessori teacher and now as a mother leads me to a deeper reverence for Maria's insights. I also discovered how much Piaget knows about who my children are and how they think.

David Elkind, in a lecture he gave to MECA-Seton students in April 1978, made an excellent comparison between Maria's and Piaget's discoveries. I highly recommend Elkind's books to you if you have not yet studied them. I have observed in my own children, and noticed in open educators all around the world, the same observations that Montessori and Piaget brought to us.

I would like to suggest to you today a real change! Not in the apparatus, but in the relationship of ourselves as educators to the child and to the child–apparatus relationship. I call it the dynamic approach. Let's discuss it.

I became very interested in developing techniques for conceptual learning, Recently, I attended several workshops and had several new experiences. It seems to me that Montessorians are being distracted from the apparatus and bringing junk into their class in the name of science.

Piaget did not build a curriculum; he did not prepare a class. The ones following him today and naming their experiences "Piaget classes" are doing him a disservice, diminishing the impact of his genius by superimposing the poverty of their own attempts at curriculum building.

I saw in many classes the addition of many materials, for instance, in math, to "complete" the Montessori set! My own classroom and educational analysis is that the set of math materials, for instance, is fully adequate. We just need to address it with an alert educational eye, following the child's discoveries, not imposing rules and skills.

I remember visiting a class in which the Pink Tower was put in a basket to follow Piaget's insight, in an attempt to be modern, to let the child construct his world—in this case, to discover gradation. I observed for many hours the experiments the child did with the "basket tower" were absolutely the same as a 2½-year-old would have done in a so-called "orthodox" environment—total play in search of seriation.

Maria was not an epistemologist, but she built a curriculum and built a school that created an impact in the world of education.

Our task as aware teachers today in Montessori Children's Houses is to continue her work, advance it, and include serious study of Piaget, as she would have done if she were still alive with us. We must revitalize our apparatus, revitalize our view of how to provoke thinking.

We do not need to play modern. What we need is to convert ourselves to the needs of the child. To improve ourselves we need to study the best scientists of today and, thus, better understand the world of the child.

What we need to change is not the environment or the apparatus of the Children's House. These are our best legacy. *We need to change our understanding of how to present reality to the child.* We need to study what the child understands of this reality and how to provoke him to higher levels of thinking.

Constance Kamii and Rheta DeVries (1976) propose some interesting points in their NAEYC publication *Piaget, Children and Number.* I would like to stress some of their points:

The child constructs his own concepts. We can encourage him. How?

- Think about number all the time.
- Develop language that provokes logical quantification and comparison of groups.

For instance, it is so simple to say:

> "Bring just enough cups for everybody at your table" instead of "Bring six cups," and instead of having a very good assistant that counts all the cups so you have exactly a controlled environment with as many cups as children.

Other ways to develop number concepts—use the following phrases:

- Do we have enough for everybody to have one?
- Do we have too many cups?
- Do you have as many cups (or the same amount or the same number) as I have?
- Who has more?
- Bobby has less (or fewer) than you do.

Using all aspects of our language, employ comparisons and logical mathematical expressions, instead of simple counting. The more the child is active in creating sets, the more he builds his number concepts.

Make the passage from *simple abstraction*, where all that the child must do is focus on a certain physical property of the object and ignore the others, to *constructive abstraction*, which involves the creation of mental relationships between and among objects. It is vital for us. For instance, our decimal system apparatus gives the child a possibility to work in the simple abstraction level up to one thousand or forty-five thousand (the latter in the classroom where forty-five thousand cubes still exist). But numbers are learned, *not by abstraction from sets* that are already made, but *by abstraction as the child constructs relationships*. Because these relationships are created by the mind, it is possible to think of numbers such as one million even if we have never seen one million objects in a set. Number concepts come when the child is ready to *order* mentally. The child has the concept of number when he is able to see the relationship of *class inclusion* that exists in a quantity: to cognitively understand the concept of the number of what "three" is. Three mentally includes one in two, two in three. Three is a quality that does not exist in any object by itself, but rather in an expressed relationship that is formed with other objects.

Piaget's theory of the logical mathematical nature of number is in contrast with the common assumption that number concepts can be taught. They have to be constructed by the child's own processes.

I teach a child that this is "a chair" (simple abstraction)—observation plus arbitrary social transmission: chair. For example, I observe a chair, I feel and move the chair, I memorize the word "chair," and in the future I can identify other "chairs" based on this simple abstraction.

Number concepts include more, much more, than this simple abstraction. They involve the creation of mental relationships. Number cannot be abstracted by simple abstraction. The child needs to create relationships in his mind. Encourage children in general, to put all kinds of events, objects, and actions into relationships.

I am always amazed when analyzing the way we prepare teachers. We see some teacher education courses proposing that first-year students create new materials and then use them in their classes. My aim in teacher education is, instead, to have the student teacher relating to the apparatus in a creative way. The only way in which I would accept a teacher education course to propose that a student teacher should build a new material would be for her to discover, through her work in the classroom, how children think. Then she can go back to the regular Montessori apparatus and improve the presentation to the child.

IV. In Conclusion

I would like to emphasize today the role of the apparatus in the development of thinking and the very special place of the educator in introducing the child to reality through the apparatus. I would like to share with you some points that I feel need further reflection:

1. The classical presentations and the need for reconstruction. Do we address the physical knowledge level only? Do we provoke the child's thinking in the effort to discover reality? Are we aware that no cognitive development exists merely through sensorial stimulation?

2. The role of the teacher (directress) has been too often presented as that of a passive observer, indirectly teaching. How to describe

the real educator, capable of introducing reality to the child and respecting the child's work while he is constructing his own concepts? More and more I see the need of educators who are extremely developed intellectually and well-balanced emotionally to teach little people.

3. My third and last point is quite paradoxical. The more we discover the apparatus, the more we need it as it is. Let's rephrase: We do not need to add to the apparatus. It has in itself quite a complete set for the child's construction of reality. We can have Montessori without walls, without shelves, and without all the materials as long as we try to learn from all of the great educators who preceded us.

Thank you.

☙

A MONTESSORI ALL-DAY PROGRAM

Introduction, overview, and interview from an article published in AMS's publication *The Constructive Triangle* (used with permission)

1981, 1999, 2014

by Celma Pinho Perry

Introduction (for a presentation given in 2014)

Seton was built to serve the parents who were carefully studying and looking for an up-to-date early childhood education program.

For the founding parents, Montessori was their choice, and so Seton Montessori School was built.

From 1965 to 1972 we had children attending half day classes — a.m. or p.m., with a choice to add a lunchtime program from 11:30–1:30 p.m. We had a three-acre campus, and a beautiful Children's House, built for children from 2–6 years old. The year of 1973 brought a necessary evolution: parents needed a longer program.

Children were comfortable and happy at Seton. Slowly we decided to help the working parents and receive children from 7:00 am–5:00 p.m.

Our staff needed specific training. We were used to eating meals together, but did not know how to offer naps, how to balance activities to have our school really functioning as a Children's House all day long.

Once the decision was made with the faculty, we did our research and we started the 1973 school year with fifteen all-day children. Now, in 2014, we have over sixty Early Childhood students (plus more in our Infant, Toddler, and Elementary programs) proud of their environments, involved in their intellectual development, aware of the others, open to deeper friendships, happy to be in a place specially designed for their age, their size, their culture.

One of my best experiences took place when a university professor came to visit Sue's all-day classroom for an afternoon. Dr. David Misner was very accustomed with observing environments, and he concentrated on the Math materials designed by Maria Montessori and so beautifully presented by the teacher to a 4 ½-year-old girl who was excited to complete a multiplication problem. But his eyes caught Ralph, working on a rug on the floor with a set of pictures, placing them in two columns: Rembrandt and Renoir. Dr. David waited. When the distribution was finished, he asked Ralph, "How do you like Rembrandt?" Ralph answered in a very relaxed way: "I love the light in the pictures, but Renoir's colors are so beautiful." Dr. David could not believe that a 5-year-old child was more able than most of his university students in the analysis of art.

In the all-day classroom, the doors open at 7:00 a.m. with Montessori staff members already present. Breakfast is organized, and each child who wants to eat chooses food and sits at the table, beautifully set with flowers, napkins, and all the needed complements. As they finish, the children clean up, wash hands, and transition to the academic materials, choosing (very carefully) their work. The educator, as a facilitator, quietly helps each individual and probes their interests.

An overview of the All-Day Program with the Staff of Seton Montessori, (excerpted from "A Montessori All-Day Program" by Celma Pinho Perry with Seton staff, originally published in *The Constructive Triangle*,

Vol. 8, No. 4, copyright American Montessori Society 1981. Used with permission.)

When Eric (age 3) and Patricia (age 5) arrive at the Children's House, the first thing they do is make toast and prepare cereal for their own breakfast. They are helped by Debbie, one of the all-day Montessori trained staff.

Then they go out quickly to help feed Nanny, the goat, as well as the chickens, and Charlie the rabbit. Before they leave the animal coop, they search near the chicken roost and find two eggs. Later these will be used in the baking project.

When they get back to the kitchen, the other children are clearing away breakfast dishes, stacking the dishwasher and sweeping the floor. Eric gets a dustpan and brush because he enjoys cleaning activities. Patricia joins the older children preparing celery and cheese for snack time.

By now, Sue, the teacher, has arrived, and the line activity is started. Children run, skip, hop, and gallop; the line gives focus to their movements and helps build self-control.

There is a brief welcoming song when all the children are present and Sue introduces an activity which some of the older children will enjoy—polishing a hubcap. The children choose their first activity, and a regular Montessori morning has begun.

Toward the end of the morning, Patricia comes and tells young Eric, "Good, our two names are on the lunch helpers list." Eric puts his work away. Patricia, who had just started a word-building exercise, pulls the rug to a corner where she can resume her work during naptime. (She is too old now for a nap.)

They join two other children tidying up the kitchen and setting tables. Then they go back and join the other children on the line. They are just in time for the Silence Game. Sue asks each child to close his eyes while all listen to the music box. They listen to the tune and, when it's over, they hum it very softly with her. It's a new tune so they hum it several times and Sue tells them the name.

At lunch, Maria and Debbie serve vegetable soup. As the children finish, they stack their soup bowls near the dishwasher and pick up a glass of milk and a plate of beef goulash with vegetables. These are taken back to their places.

The emphasis is on making mealtime a family experience with all the rules of Grace and Courtesy. Older children help the younger ones. Tables are set with real silverware, real dishes, real flowers, and a minimum of plastic.

"Do you want Beethoven's *Pastorale* or Saint Saëns' *The Carnival of the Animals* for background music today?"

Eric and Patricia go outside after lunch to enjoy the balance beam, chinning bar, and sandbox. The after-lunch helpers will sweep the floor, stack the dishwasher, and leave the kitchen neat and tidy for the afternoon cooking project.

Eric finds a friend who helps him ride a tricycle. He needs some help with this. Other children dig in the garden and harvest the ripening cucumbers, zucchini, and other squash. There are a couple of large pumpkins to be harvested a few days before Halloween.

Halloween and Thanksgiving are big events, celebrated with all the staff and as many parents as can come. But, snow time is what is enjoyed most — the sleds come out and the children make "angels in the snow" and sometimes igloos.

After a time outdoors, Eric comes in and goes to the nap room, which has been darkened. The cots are ready, so he gets his sheet and blanket and koala bear, and he makes his bed. He got messy playing outside, so he washes up, comes back, lies down, and falls asleep quickly.

Patricia comes in and goes to the line where the "composer of the week" is being introduced. It is George Gershwin, and Patricia really enjoys *Rhapsody in Blue*. She tells Sue, "It makes me see pictures in my mind."

Nicole comes in to give a French lesson, after which Patricia takes out her rug with the word-building she had begun earlier. Her written paper goes into her folder, which will be shown to her parents at the next conference.

While the younger children nap, the older ones work at more advanced activities in biology, geography, Math, and Language. The pace is leisurely, the classroom is half-empty, and the teacher may take them on occasional rambles in the nearby woods, a trip to the zoo or nature center, or just introduce a new art activity.

At snack time, the nappers reappear, and all the children discuss the special art or baking project, which will take up most of the rest of the afternoon. Today they learn how to make zucchini bread with eggs from their coop and zucchini from their garden.

Now it's time for the "short-day" (3:00 p.m. dismissal) children to go home. While they are gathering in the hallway, the All-Day children go to the last line of the day. Bee Jay has just arrived and is fresh to supervise the activity—a puppet play by Patricia and a friend. They use hand puppets from the French lesson and, although the play would hardly win an award, the audience cheers loudly.

After snack, the children go outdoors to their favorite play areas; however, before 5:00 p.m., the children put away all outdoor materials and toys and return to the library area for a quiet reading time until they are picked up. The late afternoon helper, Yvonne, a high school student, enjoys reading to the children. Most children curl up to listen; Patricia prefers to work with the bead cabinet and invites a friend to join.

When the cars come, Eric's and Patricia's parents hear a long, jumbled story about eggs, chickens, zucchini bread, sand castles, and climbing trees. It may take the rest of the evening to sort out the events of a full Montessori All-Day program.

In an interview, *The Constructive Triangle* asked Celma Pinho Perry, Director of the MECA-Seton All-Day program, how it evolved. Here, in part, is her reply:

I have been building this program since 1972 at Seton Montessori School in Clarendon Hills, and more recently at MECA's other lab school in Barrington.

The program originated because I dreamed of recreating the situation I lived in during my internship at Grandbourg, near Paris, under Lubienska de Lenval in the 1950s. It was a real Children's House, a boarding school for children from 4 to 14 years of age.

The strength of the experience was a program based on children's needs, trusting children, instead of a bureaucratic organization to be followed by children. For twenty-four hours a day the atmosphere was happy and free. Children chose their own activities, developed at their own pace and slowly discovered the whole of Creation.

There were long afternoon walks with Lubienska in the nearby Fontainebleau forests, where we picked berries, climbed trees, and collected leaves and branches to be woven into baskets. I remember the "Silence Games" where children would eagerly discover all the shades of green in the forest. Trainee-teachers were expected to observe the children constantly and to refrain from interfering. It was a place for children to grow, happy, curious, fully human, free of aggressive patterns so often developed by so-called teachers in other schools.

Q: What are the leading ideas that gave birth to this All-Day program?

A: The key is quality training of the director and staff. With the All-Day experience, as with family life, we cannot cheat. It is serious work. A three-hour nursery school can be artificially organized, but the All-Day program demands your whole soul, all of your Montessori understanding.

There are four main points for this specific experience:

1. An extended family atmosphere, where we share with parents their difficult task.

2. A Montessori atmosphere all day, requiring Montessori-trained teachers in supervision at all times.

3. The prepared environment must be comprised of several rooms within the allotted space.

4. A harmonious schedule and an intelligent curriculum.

Q: **OK, that sounds simple. But let's go back to the first point. How do you go about creating a collaborative atmosphere with parents?**

A: It is vital that busy parents feel welcome. We maintain an open-door policy so that parents can observe their child, visit with the teacher, spend time with the child when there is an opportunity, and thus share in giving care.

Parents know we admire them, their efforts; we know how difficult it is to "parent." They can count on us.

They are involved informally with real situations—materials workshops, brunches, outdoor cleanup days, parent nights, etc. Whenever it is appropriate, we provide a staff member to be with the children during the parent activity. As the parents become more involved, they come to trust us and to grow in the relationship with their own child. The "extended family" becomes an enrichment for parents as well as children.

Q: **When you said "Montessori All-Day," I think of an article I saw that stressed how Montessori training is mainly geared to the classroom. This "school of thought" would have children in a Montessori atmosphere for a few hours each day and in the day-care situation (with lower-paid personnel) for the rest of the time. Is your Montessori All-Day possible in today's world?**

A: Maria Montessori began her life-work in a daycare situation and transformed it. We must do no less! Those persons to whom you refer must have forgotten to read Montessori's *The Secret of Childhood* and *The Child in the Family*.

I feel that too many people look upon Montessori primarily as a technique for "school" hours. We see it very differently, and we train teachers to follow the philosophy and implement the techniques of Montessori throughout the child's day.

In Europe I never visited a Montessori school where children went for fewer than seven hours. The three-hour program commonly found in America is, as Dr. Nancy Rambusch has said, an adaptation of Montessori to the American way of doing things following the success of the nursery school model of the 1950s.

Q: **Could you explain what you mean by an environment specially prepared for the Montessori All-Day?**

A: Just follow the children! When children spend most of their waking hours in the Children's House, the environment must be prepared for this. Several rooms within the space must be available—living room, kitchen, nap room, soft corner, play room—all organized according to Montessori techniques, so that a child can move from one place to another and choose his activities in accordance with his own rhythm.

A natural outdoor environment is also most important. I like sandboxes, puppet theaters, construction materials, and workbenches with tools adapted for the young child. Each child takes a nap and should have his own blanket, sheet, and teddy bear for naptime.

Q: **One last question. How do you define "harmonious schedule" and "intelligent curriculum?"**

A: May I use a paradox? If you want success in Montessori All-Day, you must plan strictly and continuously—and yet, you must continuously accommodate to the child's needs.

There must be a readiness to flow—to adapt to the needs of the group and to each child, but only after you have extensively planned your program. Not only must the physical environment be meticulously prepared, but you must also have a well-developed curriculum with progressive presentations for each group and for each child within the group.

Each child must feel free to accept or reject the presentations offered. You must present real options, each week, each season, and each year. Too often the child is left on his own because adults are not ready for a fruitful dialogue. Too often the same things are presented because nothing else is ready.

At MECA-Seton we have prepared our curriculum on a three-year basis, the average length of the child's stay in the Children's House. Parents are told what their child is being offered by means of a weekly newsletter, so they can deepen the experience at home. All-Day children particularly need the stimulation of well-planned presentations. This limits discipline problems encountered in daycare and home situations.

Children without an interest and intelligent goal, as well as without options, tend to become bored or "hyperactive." I personally supervise the planning curriculum and the teacher has the task of adapting it to the child's conscious or unconscious needs. Teacher and child must have fun doing what they do.

∽

CONSIDERATIONS FOR IMPLEMENTING MONTESSORI EDUCATION

An excerpt from a letter to public schools interested in starting Montessori programs

1989

by Celma Pinho Perry

My work in the public schools of Kankakee and Cairo, IL, Benton Harbor, MI, and Gary, IN started with this simple outline and grew to the formation of real public Montessori Children's Houses.

We created this program to prepare a group of teachers and aides, especially in public education, to implement the insights of Maria Montessori about how children learn. Briefly, we propose to set up a learning environment where children, in groups or singly, can experiment with the materials, can derive enjoyment from the experimentation, and through manipulation and sensory experience can derive knowledge of the world in which they live. It has been shown through research that children through the third grade are unable to grasp merely verbal teaching. To comprehend thoroughly they must be given concrete experiences, concrete materials for manipulation. Presenting numbers on a chalkboard is far less effective than providing pebbles, beads, or cubes for the children to count, add, multiply, or subtract.

It has been demonstrated that some children learn concepts very quickly while others take more time to master them. The teaching method of Maria Montessori allows the rapid learner to follow and deepen his interests, unimpeded by the rest of the group. The slower learner can build up his concepts at his own pace, helped by the physical environment and the individualized help of the teacher. Montessori education is a system where each child is to be respected as a person and given an environment that satisfies his or her inner needs.

1. All children are seen as people, therefore all children are accepted equally, with no restrictions of race, creed, or ability.

2. Since the home plays a vitally important role in the education of the child, parents will be asked to become a part of the program through personal interviews and conferences, observations, parent meetings, workshops for developing new teaching materials, and as volunteers. We advise that parents be given the opportunity to attend a Community Awareness Workshop in order to grasp the basics of a personalized education.

3. The teachers implementing the program will have specific training in Montessori techniques and environmental design, as well as in Jean Piaget's analysis of the sequence of the child's development of cognitive structures. The teachers must be prepared to go *beyond* their traditional training, while utilizing it as fully as possible. Montessori education will lead them to create materials that children can manipulate and from which they can derive important concepts.

4. The Seton Montessori Institute faculty member will provide specific instruction on the insights of Montessori and Piaget, and will prepare the accepted candidates in the methods of individualized education, at the same time respecting the curriculum proposed

by the school district. The teachers will be responsible for relating the curriculum to the method and the learning environment.

5. Curriculum and environment: In the Montessori-based approach, the environment is the curriculum. Special learning materials in Practical Life, sensory-motor education, Math, Language, art, cosmic education, geography, history, natural science, and perceptual motor development are introduced. The child is encouraged and helped to learn by experiencing and manipulating the material. As reading skills are developed, the child is introduced to a research library where projects are chosen that appeal to the child. The choice and pursuit of the projects is closely supervised by the teacher. Children may work in groups or individually, with or without the physical presence of the teacher, but always under strict guidance and control.

6. Readings are required before the course begins to enhance and enlarge the teachers' awareness of philosophy, psychology, child development, and Montessori methods.

❧

THE MONTESSORI CHILDREN'S HOUSE: PHILOSOPHICAL DIMENSIONS, PRACTICAL IMPLICATIONS, SILENCE, WONDER, NORMALIZATION

An address at the American Montessori Society National Conference

Chicago, IL • 1992

By Celma Pinho Perry

Many different ideas are going to be covered during this presentation:

The Philosophical Foundation of Education:
(Who is the person? What is life? How do we educate?)

Practical Implications and techniques:

1. The Silence Game—helping children discover life

2. Observe the child — follow the child

3. Organization of movement and education

4. Line and Exercises of Grace and Courtesy

5. Normalization

6. Normalization and internal unification

Let's consider these ideas:

The Philosophical Foundation of Education

Philosophy means "love of wisdom". Philosophy is the search for the fundamental "why." Philosophy is our seeking to discover the mystery of reality. In other words, as Professor Boehlen (1968, p. vii) used to say, "The beginning of philosophy is wonder." Wonder is the lasting source of fundamental thinking. The philosopher (the lover of wisdom) ceases to be a philosopher when he ceases to wonder.

The importance of being an educator derives from our continuous search, our continuous wonder. As Dr. Shirley Morgenthaler stated in her speech to the Chicago Metro Association of Education for Young Children educators (1992), "Children don't learn from our teaching. They catch learning from our learning."

Celma and Shirley in 2005

Practical Implications and Techniques:

1. The Silence Game — helping children discover life

Some simple exercises in the Montessori Children's House call forth a response from the whole child and create an atmosphere where children discover themselves, life around them, and other people.

My first introduction to Montessori was visiting a class of thirty children, aged three to six, who had been called for Silence. Each one had brought a chair to the line. They sat with their hands on their knees, very relaxed, very calm, and very attentive. They waited for their teacher to call them by name. I could feel the ritual, the teacher standing up, going by the door, and whispering each name.

I could not hear any sound! My ears were not ready for this careful analysis of silence. Like magic, each little one got up and very carefully stood by the teacher, turned towards the class, and happily waited for the next one to be called. They came to the teacher most carefully. Not one sound was heard because they knew how to control every little noise their feet could make.

When the last one arrived they all smiled and gently giggled. The teacher sat on a little bench and showed them some branches of trees with new leaves, as it was the beginning of spring. They were very receptive to the information. In the afternoon they were going out for a walk in the nearby forest!

This is the description of a typical Silence Game in our Montessori Children's Houses. How were the children introduced to it? Why were they so calm? I did not observe any aggression or discontent during the entire exercise. Silence is very often a discovery. "Suddenly, after climbing a mountain, I see the majestic view from the top and my lungs fill with fresh air, and I am in awe! I just look and rejoice!" (Lubienska 1957, from the Introduction)

Silence is also the result of training, one step after the other. Indeed, silence is not the absence of words.

Let's see how to introduce the Silence Game in the Children's House.

First step:

In the beginning, silence requires effort. It's a tension; it's a work. We start by encouraging each child to be very still. We must be aware of our whole body. At the line we learn how to move following a rhythm, a voice. In the Silence Game, we learn how to make our body still, able to move only when we choose to.

This first step of the Silence Game is very important. It gives direction to all our educational effort. To educate is to be with the child so he becomes aware of reality.

During this first step toward silence, the Silence Game teaches the child, "I am able to tell myself, my body, what to do."

Indeed, this capacity of making ourselves still, to do what we want, is basic. Very often the interest of life calls us and we are stopped, breathless, in awe, able to admire. Nonetheless, it is by a daily effort in knowing when to stop, when to move, in directing ourselves in a given direction that we grow.

Second step:

Once we know how to be still, we are ready for more. As we start the Silence Game, the teacher proposes, "Let's hear the voices of what is around us; let's be very still, close our eyes, and try to hear what is happening around us."

After some thirty seconds we open our eyes and listen to the children:

- The train passed
- The mailman opened the mailbox
- The neighbor's dog barked, etc.

This time, already able to be still, relax, and become attentive to the voice of what exists around each of them. Deep development is seen in this growth of the child becoming aware of himself, aware of the world around him.

In this second step, similar activities would be to bring a music box and listen to it, or to bring a clock and listen to the tick-tock, etc.; but silence goes beyond what we hear with our ears.

We can find a place where we can think by ourselves in a Children's House where children are respected and respectful. Grace and Courtesy exercises are well established, and group activities are always invitational.

Third step:

I remember the joy of the children on the day I brought a rose very carefully to the line. I brought it slowly, almost as a ritual. The children followed each of my moves. I then invited them to silence saying, "Mother's Day is this Sunday. When I see roses, I always think of my mom. I just wonder… what is my mom doing now?" I closed my eyes meditatively. They all imitated me. After almost sixty seconds I told them, "I think my mother is smiling." And slowly they started telling what they thought their mothers were doing.

We did not rush. During Silence Game, the world stops. We know we will listen to each person. We taste each experience. We enjoy thinking about Mom. All of these steps prepare the child to admire, to look beyond what she sees, to meditate.

Fourth step:

This step is very nondirective. After having often experienced silence, just sit and invite the children for silence.

I remember one year, when after two full minutes I opened my eyes and the children were still relaxed, in a certain communion with life. Little children are open to what is most important. Happy are the teachers who can touch life in them by offering an environment where they can be themselves, more and more aware of reality. I also remember what happened sometime in 1964 when I went to visit the class of Dome Petrutis at Ronald Knox Montessori School in Wilmette, IL, to supervise one of our student teachers.

It was around 9:15 a.m. when a little boy came near Dome and told her, "I want to do the Silence Game." She understood and told him, "You may do it. I will call you." The boy found a place by a table, sat down, put his hands on the table, having his whole body as in attention, with his two feet together on the floor. I was amazed! Thirty seconds, one minute, two minutes… and the boy totally still waited to be called. When Miss Petrutis finally looked at him and called his name, he answered, "Here I am," and smiled. I remembered a passage of the Bible when God called Samuel… "Samuel! Samuel!" and Samuel responded, "Here I am."

I wish to finish by reminding you of a simple story Maria Montessori told about Silence when she called the children to see a baby asleep. This reverence for life, this joy, is what education is about.

2. Observe the child—follow the child

E. M. Standing shows us how most people think of children as noisy creatures, especially if they are in a group. Many people are then surprised, he says, when Maria Montessori tells how she discovered, that deep down, children are great lovers of silence (See *The Secret of Childhood*).

To discover this we must follow the child, have a prepared environment, avoid rewards and punishments, and focus on the environment, and activities, on choosing, to satisfy the child's real needs; all that has to do with his growth, with learning, fascinates the child.

Children learn how to move among things. They become more and more agile. They rejoice in the perfection of their achievements. Maria Montessori says they discover themselves and their capacities, and slowly gain practice.

The Silence Game normalizes children. They find their peace, their joy, in listening to the world and saying "yes" to life.

3. Organization of movement and education

The child needs the adult. Alone, the child does not organize his movements. He touches everything without aim, does not stop moving, etc. An excellent example is found in the book and movie about the wild child of Aveyron, about a child who is raised without adults (Itard 1962).

The child needs the adult. The adult is there to help the child organize his movements, direct his own activity. It is the movement education—the line—that gives the Montessori child self-awareness, self-control, agility to act, grace, courtesy, and discipline.

ssori teacher gives a presentation she uses a technique ysis of movement." The line continues this technique in all activities—how to walk, how to stop, how to sit, how to jump, etc.

The line has a very specific aim in the classroom. It gives the child a chance to analyze his movements, become conscious of his power, and do with his body what he chooses.

The educated child is the child who is aware of reality and is responsible. At the line the child becomes aware of himself, aware of others, aware of the world around him, and responsible for it.

The line is not for entertaining the child, to distract or to play. The line must enrich through helping the child discover rhythm, sound, balance, etc.

We must direct the development of movement so it can be a healthy part of a healthy person.

The line became part of the Montessori method because of Maria's observations and her strong connection with the work of Edouard Séguin. Séguin worked with retarded children and learned that walking patterns are very important in the development of the child. This is why walking exercises are among the first line activities.

Maria Montessori reminds us about the attraction each young child has to walk on rails, edges of sidewalks, etc. We have all experienced this. Thus, she brought the line to the class in the form of a circle.

In order to walk on the line, children must pay attention. Slowly, the difficulty is increased to include balancing exercises and others that increase the child's posture and awareness.

Our goal is to help them focus their attention and establish a body rhythm that is regular and harmonious. This is even more important with the children who have balance difficulties. We need to help them acquire control of their body through movement. Try different rhythms. Help each child achieve. Slowly, all the other areas of development will gain from this effort.

I would like to bring you a conversation I often heard Lubienska have with the children at the line.

"Who directs your feet?" she asks.

"I do," says the child.

"How do you do it?"

"My mind tells my feet and they do it."

"Your mind? It's you! You are a strong person. You can do what you want. You are the one telling your feet to do it."

It is very important that the child realizes that he is the one in command.

As educators we are the servants, the facilitators.

4. Line and Exercises of Grace and Courtesy

To be able to direct myself, to control my movements, to choose, is a big thing. But to educate, we need to look for more: as I become more aware of myself I can become aware of others.

Create these situations for them, for example:

How to greet

How to say thank you

How to welcome a friend to your home

How to say goodbye

How to give your chair to someone who needs to sit

How to take a bus

How to clean your nose, etc.

A Children's House where a teacher is prepared to give exercises of Grace and Courtesy, where children learn how to act, how to respond in different situations, is a place where children can be happy.

Pay attention to each meal. Pay attention to guests. Pay attention to one another.

As educators we have to help the child discover the others around him.

5. Normalization

We are called to be human. All of us are able to respond on our own level, overcoming our particular difficulties.

Maria Montessori tells us in *The Secret of Childhood* (1981, 141) that we can call for "a conversion" for the child. When a swift, sometimes instantaneous change occurs, she says that these changes are always due to the same occurrence: it would not be possible to quote a single example of conversion that did not involve the concentration of activity and an interesting task.

If the child is converted by the task after he experiences the joy of work again and again, he becomes "normalized" (1981, 141).

The adult is there to constantly help in this conversion, again and again. So we are not to deny "deviations." The Montessori class is not a place for little "angels." Children that come to us with this or that habit that makes concentration and joy difficult for them must be helped. We have to constantly help the child to overcome, give chances for conversion. We must build an environment that fosters normalization as much as possible. Normalization comes through work. The normalized child is the child who is interested in life.

Respect him. Maria Montessori will tell you not to respect evil in the child. Respect the child who is interested; respect his rhythm. With the difficult child, help him again and again to convert, to find interest, to find life.

Education starts with normalization.

Signs of normalization:

- Love of order
- Love of work
- Profound spontaneous concentration

- Love of silence and of working alone

- Sublimation of possessive instinct

- Motivation by real choices

- Obedience—willingness to carry out commands

- Independence initiative

- Spontaneous self-discipline

- Joy—a mysterious happiness

We talk about normalization. "Concern for humanization leads at once to the recognition of dehumanization...." (Freire 1970, 24). As we perceive the extent of dehumanization, we ask ourselves if humanization is a viable condition. As educators we have to help the child against any oppression, any dehumanization.

Normalization is not something we acquire forever. It is an ongoing process. As an educator, my first task is to humanize, to be a facilitator of normalization.

6. Normalization and internal unification

All our progress comes from successive unifications—it is the law of growing. Let me explain:

The child brings to himself what is around him, the complex objects that he slowly understands. It is in the moment in which he has penetrated the reality of this one object that he knows it. Then he is ready for the next step, the next complexity.

The educator is a facilitator of continuous interior unifications. The child who does not grow, unifying his contact with reality, becomes either like a broken glass—pieces without reality—or he unifies himself around fantasies and fears.

The educator foresees and facilitates continuous unifications.

The importance of the educator being in continuous search, in continuous wonder, is told again in other words by Martin Buber. "Only in his whole being, and all his spontaneity, can the educator truly affect the whole being of his pupil. His aliveness streams out to them and affects them most strongly and purely when he has no thought of affecting them" (Boehlen 1968, 254).

Boehlen concludes the non-utilitarian spontaneity of authentic inspiration (wonder) is the most effective and growth-provoking discipline (1968).

Let's allow ourselves to be constantly seeking, wondering, and celebrating our joy of being.

Our students will then be introduced to reality and pass it on to the next generation.

❧

Reinventing My Professional Life: Montessori and Me

An address at the American Montessori Society National Conference

Chicago, IL • 1997

By Celma Pinho Perry

Last November, as I was passing by one of the major landmarks of our city, the Newberry Library, I saw this page of calligraphy, attributed to Gregory Norbert, OSB:

> The Color and the Texture
>
> You have added to my Being
>
> Have become a song
>
> And I want to sing it forever

This poem reminded me of the happy moment in 1956 when I met again Hélène Lubienska de Lenval in a city close to Paris. It was my first visit to a Montessori Children's House. This moment ignited in me the strong call to serve the child. My response to this call has directed me all the years of my life… even now!

I was twenty-two years old at the time. I was in the midst of a long, calm, silent, solitary retreat in which I was seeking a direction for all the "élan vital" (essence or vital force) I felt inside myself.

Our professional lives often begin with a simple call, a simple coincidence, and the fact that we accept a job or a course of study. Carl Rogers, in *On Becoming a Person*, says "what is most personal is most general" — that the moments of our life that we recognize as most personal are the ones that everyone has experienced within their own lives (1961, 26).

Let us reflect on our beginnings, the strong moments that give direction to our lives.

When did you decide to be an educator, a Montessorian?

The fact is clear, one way or another, in a certain place, at a certain time, sometimes in a very simple way, our life as educators, as Montessorians, was decided.

I am the one, who in my maturity, accepted the challenge.

Who am I?

In the middle of all we do for everybody in our family as well as in our professional life, one reality is constant: I am the one in charge of me.

In order to operate well, I must recognize my needs.

What are my needs?

What is my potential?

If I try to analyze my choice, I discover that in order to choose, in the full sense of the word, I must have knowledge of the object of my choice. I can only choose when I know.

In my life, I can't direct myself without knowing who I am, what I need, what I have.

It has been my experience as a woman having a family and working full time, that in order to survive, I can get used to almost ignoring who I am, what I need, and what my potential is. We all spend precious years of our lives just doing what is necessary for surviving, or better, for helping others, at work and at home.

The success of our lives depends on much more awareness—awareness of me, my body, and my basic needs. We are the ones in charge of ourselves. We need to pamper ourselves within the limitations of our days and our responsibilities. Most of the time we take care of everybody, but we are afraid or ashamed to take care of ourselves. I have discovered that I need to pamper myself in order to better serve.

I need to take time to taste my tea, to smell the flowers, to enjoy a laugh, to sleep enough... to be. The first person I am responsible for is myself. No excuses are accepted. I am responsible for me. (I can't say I had a car accident because I was tired. It does not diminish my responsibility. I should have either rested or not driven at all).

Once I remember asking a friend in difficulty what her interests were. She told me she was so tired and exhausted that she had none. This is often how we feel when we are fatigued. So, I asked her, "What are you able to do?" (What is your potential?) As she looked within herself and recognized her potential, she made a choice and started a new life filled with many interests.

My first responsibility is myself.

Do I know what I am?

What is the Reality I am aware of? In other words, what is my world?

What is important for me?

The more I am, the more I can give.

My Criteria for Hiring a Teacher

I was once asked about my criteria for hiring a teacher. After forty years engaged in preparing contracts, I had to thoughtfully consider my response.

1. An educator needs to be primarily a mature individual.

The adult is a person that has unified and integrated his personality. The mature adult is not like an adolescent, trying to discover himself. The Latin sense of the word "adolescence" means the person in the making, ripening to maturity; "adult" means a person completed—and we recognize that not all adults are mature (Liegé 1958, 7–9).

The child and the adolescent have moments of unification of their personality; but these moments are passages and do not last. On the other hand, the adult knows all of his potential, knows himself. He is able to concentrate, to express himself, to give himself. We can count on his coherence.

The adult has convictions. He is no longer an adolescent whose actions are based on passion and passing interests. His choices reflect the depth of his life, and he is consistent.

The adult knows he is responsible for the totality of his life. He does not change from one commitment to another without thinking. He knows that his whole life hangs together. He is faithful to his convictions and this supports the depth of his stability.

The adult is a person who is socialized. He realizes that he is part of the broader world. He is not self-centered. He is open to what exists around him.

The adult adapts to the reality of his experience. He accepts himself and others as they are. He does not live in a world filled with dreams or imagination. He accepts reality as it is and goes ahead from there.

When I think about my responsibility, opening the door of a Children's House to accept a new teacher, I see that my primary preoccupation is to see that she/he is a mature person, but a second dimension becomes necessary:

2. An educator is a mature person who wants to educate.

As adults we naturally become educators—people who bring to the new generation the best that we know. The choice of becoming a professional educator introduces a much more elaborate concept. The Greeks spoke of the pedagogue. The word comes from "paidos" (child) and "agos" (director/leader). The pedagogue was the one who directed the child.

Historically, who accomplished this function?

In Greece, a slave.

In Rome, the preceptor, also a slave.

In the Middle Ages, the poor students.

Today, all of us—teachers.

Pedagogy is the science of education. It has a practical aspect that involves skills, and even art. It also has a scientific aspect that involves knowledge, is speculative, theoretical, and needs study. The word "science" comes from the Latin *scientia*, which means "knowledge."

The pedagogical relationship exists between two unrelated people. Historically we have:

On one side, the parent who chooses the pedagogue, and pays for the work.

On the other side, the pedagogue.

The contract is between the parents and the teacher. It makes our relationship to the child always free. We are chosen by the parents, but we are free to accept or not accept the contract. This is a liberating process. No life dependence exists between the teacher and the student. The child-teacher relationship is always free, which is not the case with the parent-child relationship.

We are not a "double" of the parent. The ultimate responsibility and duty of educating is on the parent. We have a professional status only. Let us look more closely at the process of education and determine other characteristics of the educator.

We know that the principal agent of the process is the child. No one can educate another person; we can only help a person educate himself. Without the child's acquiescence the education process cannot be actualized.

So, when we seek to hire someone to be an educator, we must also assess his/her *competence*. The word "education" comes from the Latin *educere*: "to lead forth." I need to know how she can lead forth and relate to the child. The process of education is a process in which we relate to the child so she/he can become aware of Reality. Reality of things, of people, of all that exists around us:

Reality of self: who am I?

Reality of others: close to me, in my house, neighborhood, city, far away, and, within a theistic approach, Reality of the Other/God

Reality of the world around us

As the human being becomes aware of a reality, he becomes responsible for it. My task then, as an educator, is to introduce the child to the whole of reality, at his level, according to his potential, so he can become aware and thus responsible for it.

I am so interested in how different we all are from one another. In my Montessori background I have observed that each teacher, by being called to create an educational environment for the children, has before her or him a full set of personal choices. Determining what I bring to my environment reveals to me who I am. As an educator, I know I will bring to the children within the full curriculum, much of what I have become.

How can I introduce the Impressionists if I do not know them, if I did not give myself time to admire them? Within the objective choices, e.g., a box of matching pictures of works of painters (today we can even buy it ready-made), I can express the depth of my understanding of Impressionists. I remember in Amsterdam hearing a teacher tell a child about Rembrandt—the light he brought to his painting, the details, and the paint he used. Some of her own universe was being passed to this child, well beyond the simple classification of painters.

Each one of us brings to the class the world we know as well as the world in which we live. As I arrived in Chicago, in 1964, I realized the beauty of the Chicago Symphony performances. The next year, one of the board members at Seton Montessori invited me for an evening of music. This outing made me realize how much I needed music appreciation. I became a member of the Chicago Symphony, attended many lectures and performances. My earlier education was not strong enough in music appreciation. I had to enlarge my world. In the following years many of the children and staff of Seton were brought to the Petites Promenades, to the wonderful afternoons of outstanding music with Mrs. Solti. The board member who invited me in 1965 probably did not know he was deepening my world. He was giving his children a teacher who was more open to music.

Having one of our Children's Houses close to Argonne National Laboratory, (one of the laboratories that investigated atomic energy with the University of Chicago) brought an international and intellectual population of families to our suburbs in the 1960s. As those families discovered our program, it allowed us to include diverse children at Seton Montessori School.

One day this little girl told me, "We are going to travel." I asked, "Where?" She told me, "I don't remember. It is to Paris to visit *grand-maman*, or to Springfield to visit grandma." Her world was so encompassing of other languages, other cultures, and other places, just as part of her everyday reality.

We carry the dimensions of our world to our daily lives. As an educator I'm always so interested in knowing, in learning. I want to know more about people and things so I can bring a deeper understanding of life to the children.

The Process of Education

As we analyze the process of education, we see that relationships between the teacher and the child, at whatever age, are based on the patterns of the dialogue, of a conversation.

I can't find a definition for the process of education, but I can try to describe it, to reflect from different views in order to highlight the essentials of the educational process.

The educator, as the one who engages in a dialogue, is someone who knows, and has trained himself in being present to the child. Nobody can relate to someone who is not listening and engaging while he converses. Often as a child comes to us we are just somewhere else, not really listening or engaging with the child. The real educator is someone who is able to be here, now, with me. He is able to be *present*.

Often in our lives we meet people who have much information to show and tell. They talk so much that it is hard to put a word in, to share an idea with them. The educator, by contrast, is someone who is open to the life of others. The educator is not mute but listens actively to the words being said. The educator is able to listen, to wonder, and to wait for what the child is sharing. Often in the past, we thought that teachers had to know all and have all the answers. We see today the educator as a person who is able to *question with the child*.

I remember a boy coming home and telling his father, "The teacher told us today about butterflies." This could have been the end of the conversation, but the educator in the parent responded, "I wonder how much we could find out about a butterfly." A mutual dialogue of months of questioning the art world, natural science books, and the world of poetry, brought these two people to a real interest and awareness of butterflies. The educator is not someone who knows all: "butterflies are this or that." *The educator is the one who questions with the child, who discovers with the child all the dimensions of reality.*

A Candidate's Level of Montessori Experience

When I am asked to recommend someone as an educator for a Children's House, it is not only necessary that I assess her maturity and her strength as an educator, but I must also analyze her Montessori philosophy and her Montessori experience in depth.

I remember many years ago as I directed a Montessori elementary school in Brazil, some of the ten-year-old students came into my office. They had been in the Children's House since preschool. They had a question about the new teacher in social studies: how could I have hired her? I started explaining all I knew about this person—her degrees in geography from an outstanding university, etc. One of the girls looked at me and said, "This is exactly our problem: she knows it all. She just told us in thirty minutes everything about Japan and now told us to read and memorize for a test." Another girl added, "Couldn't she just gather us and tease our appetite about Japan, give a bibliography, and let us search? Today, I hate Japan. Send this 'good teacher' to another school. We do not need her."

In fact, this young woman was very capable in geography, but was not a Montessorian. I made a mistake in hiring her. I tried to be more cautious after that. We learn Montessori techniques by studying and becoming immersed in them.

What can I do to know a person's level of Montessori understanding?

1. Know where she/he was prepared as a Montessorian—when and by whom.

I remember one of my first meetings in Chicago with Mario Montessori. I had received a very good letter from him. He wondered why I wouldn't come to Association Montessori Internationale (AMI) in the United States instead of the American Montessori Society (AMS). He reminded me that Lubienska de Lenval worked with Montessori and that Pierre Faure was a wonderful educator, but he questioned some of the people calling themselves Montessorians in the United States and urged me to be careful.

I know what he meant. I chose AMS because I wanted, as Maria Montessori did in her time, to be very open to research and very adaptable to new needs. I believe in a strong understanding of the philosophy and of the message Maria Montessori proposed. I am very much against eclecticism (a little bit of the best of everything). I believe in being very open but very aware of my Montessori direction and do not wish to compromise it.

The place where we receive our first Montessori teacher preparation is very important—the seminars, advanced work and contacts, and visits compliment it.

2. Try to observe the person in action or to know about the Children's House: Where was she a student teacher (intern)?

This is very important since we tend to follow what we have observed in our first experience.

Other experiences she has had; i.e., other Children's Houses where she worked or is now working.

3. When I can't observe the person directly, it is been my experience that talking with someone I trust who has visited her place can be very helpful, beyond letters of recommendation.

Most times when we hire someone without careful analysis, we get both of us in trouble! When the philosophy is similar and the experiences parallel, we can expect good adjustment and interactive growth for the faculty and the new teacher.

As a Montessori educator in charge of others you must be a mature adult Montessorian who can survive, grow, and become the full person you are called to be.

Each day I must constantly evaluate my professional life. As routine gets established and tiredness moves into my daily life, I learned to find a new interest, and a new professional face. A good example was my trip to Reggio Emilia, Italy, in 1984. Often, in conversations with people who criticized Montessori, I heard, "Children need to be more creative" or "Montessori sometimes stifles life." I was getting discouraged. The observation of the Reggio Emilia classes in Italy awoke in me a real, new interest. I confronted possibilities for helping children express, invent, and discover by *themselves*. I analyzed the Reggio techniques. At the end of a three-year process, I am more of a Montessorian because I am more attentive to the child's possibilities of expression (Reggio Emilia teaches us this so well). I recognized the advantage of a Montessori environment that contains a whole curriculum at the child's fingertips, offering quality and choice at any time of the day, not only during a "project time." Reggio Emilia renewed my professional life by awakening in me again how to:

Converse with the child

Promote spontaneous communication

Develop exchange and spirit of collaboration

I renew my profession, and myself, not by looking for a contract that promises more pay with fewer hours of work, or something similar. I renew myself when all the aspects of my personality discover a new angle, become fascinated with a new question—I think of Maria Montessori's comments about the teacher in the chapter "Critical Considerations" in *The Discovery of the Child* (1967, 4–5). I would say: I renew myself when I am again like the scientist ready *to give all I am* to serve the child.

It is only when I allow myself to focus, when I somehow lose myself, that I get all I need. It is in giving that we receive: I become centered and life makes sense again. The balance of my professional life depends on the here and now of my commitment. My commitment depends on the here and now of my interest. The only things I can humanly do to reinvent my professional life are to patiently allow myself to focus, to discover new interests and new fascinations. It is not necessary to change professions or jobs. It is necessary to renew, reinvent, and redirect my most personal life.

I heard from a friend that once, before starting a battle, Napoleon was asked by a friend, "How do you win battles?" He stared, stared again, and responded, "Je m'engage et puis on voit le resultat." This translates to: "I engage all I am in it, and then I look at the result." As we choose to be in the "battle," let's just engage ourselves—all we are—and then look back and celebrate.

This also makes me think about the story of a workman sweating as he chiseled stones by the river. Someone stopped and asked him, "What are you doing?" Without hesitation he responded, "I am building a cathedral!"

The beginning of philosophy is wonder. The beginning of life is wonder! To reinvent myself, I have to build within me a new sense of wonder.

∝

THE ART OF MENTORING: PASSING THE MONTESSORI MESSAGE TO THE NEXT GENERATION

An address at the American Montessori Society 40th National Seminar

New York, NY • March 2000

by Celma Pinho Perry

Today we are going to discuss a topic that becomes more fascinating to me each day—the art, the techniques, of mentoring.

As I analyze my forty-five years of involvement in Montessori education, more specifically in teacher education, I see these years filled with the need to pass a message to others: What is the essence of Montessori, and how to assist others as they receive the information? Included within the message is the need to initiate them into the art of being, of being a Montessorian.

For me, the art of mentoring student teachers is based on:

1. My own discovery of education as an aid to life, to real life.

2. My observation that the encounter with Reality stimulates, uplifts, normalizes... a mentor must help to provoke it, thus awakening awareness.

I met Nancy Rambusch (our AMS founder) in 1964. We talked for a long time about my mentor, Lubienska de Lenval, whose books Nancy wanted me to translate from French into English.

Lubienska was a person with a very clear goal. She understood children. With Montessori, she discovered how to give children a sense of personal dignity through their involvement with their work. She had a profound respect for the child as a person, as well as for the child's potential. Lubienska was totally immersed in the experience she was living. From the first contact with her to every little detail, I felt she was a person with a goal, totally immersed and involved in what she was doing. She was very demanding, but sensitive to what she observed: the joy of a child, the discovery of a young teacher.

She was a contemplative person, capable of losing herself in the experience she was involved in. Somehow nothing else was important but the object before her. She had a certain tenacity, a stubbornness.

Through Lubienska I observed again and again the experience of "flow" that Mihaly Csikszentmihalyi (pronounced "chick-sent-mee-hali") describes and studies (1990). David Kahn wrote a foreword entitled "Finding Flow in Montessori" for a 1997 issue of *The NAMTA Journal*: he says, "Finding flow in Montessori reactivates the vision of education as Montessori called it—'an aid to life.'"

What else would education be? The art of living, of being fully involved in reality, attracted by the object before us, constantly searching, constantly relaxing, enjoying the pinnacle climbed.

One of my first experiences with Lubienska was during a long walk up a hill. When we were tired from the climbing, we stopped and sat, enjoying the sunset. She had explained Silence in her book, *Le Silence: À l'Ombre de la Parole* (1955, from the Introduction, translation mine):

She wrote:

> *In the beginning Silence is a discovery, like discovering a mountain, or poetry: sense of achievement in confronting a new reality before which everything that is fake disappears: joyful energy inviting the whole being to a new happy effort.*

She also wrote (1955, from the Introduction):

> *We discover silence in successive levels.*

- *At the physical level, while our lungs are filled with pure fresh air, our nerves tingle, our muscles are strengthened, and we feel our bodies pulsating along with the life of the universe.*

- *At the mental level, like at the completion of an arduous task, our thoughts master the intellectual horizon and, seized with wonder, rest quietly.*

- *At the spiritual level, when, beyond reasoning and feelings, the spirit accepts and touches Life!*

> *Aside from those exceptional experiences where Silence takes us over, it must be conquered through effort.*

I recognized what had happened to me that day on the long walk up the hill with Lubienska: I was touched by Silence.

Years later, when Nancy Rambusch came to lecture at MECA-Seton, she asked me, "Are you aware that along with *information*, teaching Montessori, philosophy, pedagogy, discussing child development, asking for assignments, albums, etc., you are most interested in initiating the art of being a Montessorian in your students?"

On that day in 1973, I realized that I had a commitment beyond the sharing of important information necessary to prepare teachers. I was committed to passing to the new generation the core of my life's search: The constant search to answer the question "What is reality?", and to enjoy it and to celebrate it, in the classroom, in my home, and with each child.

Lubienska also wrote *L'Education de L'Homme Conscient* (The Education of the Aware Person).

Through my readings and observations of Lubienska's work, I learned what I have taught for the past forty-five years, that to educate is to be with the other in a relationship that allows the discovery of reality and its consequence: responsibility for this reality. When we are aware, we become responsible.

Our life within the Children's House is to create an environment where the child can truly discover reality (knowing, that once the child discovers reality, he becomes responsible for it):

His own reality: who he is;

The reality of things, of the cosmos;

The reality of others;

And, in a theistic approach, the reality of God as the Other.

This process makes me think about two children's books I often read with my own two children:

1. *The Little Prince* by Antoine de Saint-Exupéry: the discovery of his Rose, and the responsibility for her.

2. *The Velveteen Rabbit* by Margery Williams: the discovery of what it means to be real.

I see our life inside the Montessori environment as a powerful experience of discovering reality with the child, from the water that comes from the faucet, cold, fresh, and lovely, to the experience of each material:

Sensorial:	what is soft, what is rough
Mathematical:	what is addition
	experience of putting together
	a square root
Geometric:	equivalences
	("This rectangle is equivalent to this triangle")

Language: I will never forget the experience of Claudia, a four-year-old child. During a reading game she discovered what is asked of her and she did it: "Eat the egg."

Some years ago, one of my former students at Seton in Clarendon Hills tragically died. I was asked to give the eulogy. Could I do it? I discovered I could do it because I had experienced with him the joy of becoming one with reality. I had observed some beautiful "flow" experiences. I even had it on film: his eagerness to learn how to tie, and, as I presented it, his joy at mastering it.

Montessori education gave me, personally, the possibility of living a very complete experience—of passing to the other all that I am, all I discovered, all I live. I chose Montessori because of this.

As an educator in the Montessori environment, I have only one goal: to bring the child individually, on his own, to discover life and discover the reality of everything he touches.

I remember Lubienska and the effort necessary to get to this high level of living, so I try to have a well-prepared environment. I try to be totally present in it, to be open to each child, in each activity she chooses and then let her go to discover on her own.

AMS recommends that the faculty of teacher education programs must have their university credentials as Montessori teachers with a minimum of five years of experience working with children. How important this is!

In his book, *Educating the Reflective Practitioner*, Donald A. Schön of MIT comments: "The most important ideas of professional practice lie beyond the conventional boundaries of professional competence.... " (1987).

Outstanding practitioners are not said to have more professional knowledge than others, but more wisdom, talent, intuition, and artistry.

From the very beginning of my career as a teacher/educator, I understood what Schön recommends: that students cannot be taught, but they can be coached. They can be stimulated, called to higher levels of experience.

1. By what we are, or by living with us in some way. A teacher must open the student to become more what she/he is called to be, beyond mere information.

2. By the quality time that we spend with them, opening new doors: e.g., "Did you notice that every number multiplied by itself makes a square?" "When multiplied by another number, it is always a rectangle." Table of Pythagoras, giving to the student time to reflect, to play with the object before him, to discover.

The mentor is not interested in covering chapters of a book or of a curriculum. We all must try to be like Socrates, going around town asking questions that provoke thought. The mentor is present to the Metanoia (from the Greek meaning "change of attitude and life direction"), to the conversion. Students can be coached, stimulated, and called to a higher level of professional and human development.

The mentor is as the philosopher, capable of wonder.

Philosophy starts with wonder;

Mentorship starts with wonder;

Mentorship is an art.

THE IMPORTANCE OF BEGINNINGS

An address for the Opening Session of the AMS Annual Teacher Education Committee Meeting

Las Vegas, NV • November 2001

By Celma Pinho Perry

Today it is a joy to address one more opening of the meeting of the Teacher Education Committee of AMS.

Today is a new start. As all beginnings, it raises questions. We do not know, we wonder what this meeting will bring to life.

Today is a new beginning for the TEC.

> *All beginnings are fundamentally mysterious. Beginning implies the emergence of something that has not yet existed in this way. Every true beginning has a creative moment for it brings something new into being. There is novelty, spontaneity, originality, and creativity in every real beginning. The reality of beginning is a phenomenon of profound mysteriousness and baffles the mind, which is still open to experience and capable of wondering.* (Boehlen 1968, 53)

Let us today, together, renew our deepest commitments to education. Our adult students, the Montessorians of tomorrow, depend on the quality of our decisions today; they depend on the quality of our teaching, of our work.

Let us commit ourselves to the depth of Montessori's views and as well to the input of today's research. Let us serve our student teachers with a solid formation and, as Nancy Rambusch often reminded us, a solid initiation in the world of observing, following the child, or committing ourselves to serving life.

This body must have rules, documents, demands, but let us go beyond them. We need a substructure of rules, but we cannot be bound by them. We cannot hide behind them.

Today is a new beginning.

Let us, in our teamwork, receive and give. We are all different. We come from different backgrounds. We had different formations. Let us, under the leadership of AMS, with our different pasts, bring to life a teacher education program that serves the child. We should follow these insights of Montessori that sometime in our career we "touched," and now we must actualize day after day.

Let us commit ourselves to more studying. Let us accompany research, help the ones who can do it, and so move with the educational process as Maria did in her fifty years of work in education.

And remember, as Martin Buber tells us, "Only in his whole being, in all his spontaneity can the educator fully affect the whole being of his pupil…. his aliveness streams out to them and affects them most strongly and purely when he has no thought of affecting them" (Boehlen 1968, 254).

Indeed, we educate, we direct our courses, with what we are.

Let's work! Let's play! Let this day be a new beginning for the direction of our programs! We work to be the best for the children in the whole world!

ॐ

THE OUTDOOR ENVIRONMENT IN MONTESSORI WRITINGS AND TRADITION

An address to Seton Montessori Institute, Administrators Paraprofessional Session

August 2001

By Celma Pinho Perry

The prepared environment is one of the central focal points of Montessori's scientific pedagogy. Indoors or outdoors, it incorporates the care of the curriculum.

As McLuhan (1964) says, "The medium is the message."

Typically, as we observe the child, we create an environment where she can become aware of reality and be called to develop her skills. The environment must be attractive, simple, and natural. Activities appropriate for each age level must be proposed and presented beautifully.

The educator is a guide, or a facilitator. He introduces the child to the activity, and the child is free to choose what, when, and how long he "plays" or "works" with it.

The play of the child is his work; the work of the child is his play.

The educator gently, respectfully creates an atmosphere of freedom and responsibility.

A socialization process is always present, as the children of different ages (mixed-age groups of 3–6 , 6–9 , or 9–12) and capabilities interact spontaneously.

All the group activities are by invitation. Those who want to join in may do so. The ones who do not choose to come will indirectly relate to it and probably choose the activity at another time. They are free to pursue their own interest without interruptions, while the group is involved in something else. The indoor prepared environment interacts continuously with the outdoor prepared environment. The child is able to go from inside to outside as conditions allow, and always with the presence of an adult.

***

In the different Montessori Children's Houses or Infant-Toddler communities, the educator will be attentive to seek and create an outdoor environment, giving to children possibilities of Montessori work outside. This includes opportunities for gardening, exercise, movement, Practical Life activities, and giving the preparation of the outdoor space the same precision as we do for the indoor environment.

In large outdoor environments, Maria Montessori proposes that each class is to have its own outdoor environment, and from there go to the larger garden or orchard.

Each class is to be an independent unit—a Children's House or an Infant-Toddler community. Large gatherings are not considered educational for this age group.

When a Children's House does not have an outdoor area, the educator will look for a possibility of walks or use of a park, and will bring some materials to the park (when allowed) to promote appropriate activities for the age group. Examples are a rake, a basket, etc.

When the Children's House has an outdoor area, Montessori activities are incorporated in very creative ways. Beyond gardening, raking, walking, a balance board, and other physical activities like climbing, throwing, catching, working with ropes, etc., we see in our classes:

- Carrying from one side to the other: bricks, stones, bags of sand
- Sifting soil
- Climbing trees, stepladders, etc.
- Washing windows, walls, etc.
- Polishing doors, doorknobs, cars, bikes, etc.
- Brushing or scrubbing stones, tires, etc.
- Cleaning, cutting vegetables, fruits, etc.

Gardens for very young children have been incorporated, whenever possible, with small interesting walks, birdhouses, birdbaths, chimes, little houses where children can sit and have a snack, sweep, change water in vases, open and close drapes, etc. A tool shed is often necessary, with a place for each instrument or activity. The tools must be available to be taken by the child and brought back at the end of the activity.

The genius of the educator is to incorporate all the necessary exercises and materials that a child of this age is capable of doing in order to maintain his physical and mental development while in the outdoor environment. Natural materials and color schemes should be used (often the different manufacturers paint their equipment in bright colors to attract the children's interest, while in Montessori the attraction must be to the beauty of the natural environment, and when we install equipment and materials they should match with the natural surroundings).

In today's world, we see the need to give our sedentary children more movement. Our awareness of the relationship between movement and intellectual development brought us to adapt a perceptual motor development program with a Montessori perspective—allowing children some choices, as well as adult observation of each child's development and appropriate support of gross motor development.

We have types of activity "stations":

Body awareness

Balance

Locomotion

Non-locomotion

Tracking

Equipment for each area is prepared according to the age of the group. Each station is monitored by one adult (parent, student teacher) at an assigned time during the day. Children come to the activities spontaneously, choosing the activity they prefer, as the adult in charge observes the performance and assists growth. If a child does not choose an activity consistently, she will be invited to it, in order to overcome the difficulty and face the challenge.

Periodically tests are made (through observation) to see the developmental level, and help the child with equilibrium and agility appropriate for their age.

During the winter these activities can be done indoors, always respecting the child's choice of activity.

If you enter a Children's House, you will see a total environment where the child can say, as Carl Rogers (1961, 22) proposes:

I can trust my experience. Here I feel I can be myself.

A place where the child can become peacefully, without interferences, the person he or she is called to be.

This is but a short overview of outdoor considerations. Children need so much movement! For more information and techniques on the importance of movement, please see the well-detailed Seton Montessori Institute publication *Perceptual Motor Development* by Desmond Perry (1975, 2010).

THE GREAT FRIENDSHIPS: ACROSS CONTINENTS, OVER TIME, LIVING MONTESSORI

Accepting the AMS Living Legacy Award at the American Montessori Society 45th National Conference

Chicago, IL • March 31, 2005

By Celma Pinho Perry

As I see all of you here today, once more I realize all the links that bind us together as educators.

Slowly, we become, we become through our encounters: no one is an island! We need *the other* to become ourselves. It's in the depth of personal encounters that we become the person, the educator we are called to be.

It's a slow process! It was while studying Martin Buber that I discovered how much my life was a constant reflection of my relationships:

I to THOU, I to IT

Indeed, each encounter throughout these fifty years of adulthood made me who I am and opened me up to life!

I arrived in Europe in 1952, still a joyful and a lively teenager! The days were long. I remember my mentor, Mère Marie, going to the garden with me while I jumped rope until I was tired enough to go to sleep. It was under her shadow that Hélène Lubienska de Lenval, the assistant of Maria Montessori during the 1930s, met me as I observed children at work. Sensing my interest, she followed my development as an educator until she died in Belgium a few months after my last visit. I discovered Montessori's thoughts and work while with her and her students.

Most encounters are not planned. They just happen! Father Pierre Faure, a Jesuit, arrived in Brazil and looked for someone to direct a demonstration class in the teacher education seminar he passionately directed. I was just twenty-four years old and I had never done anything like this before.

I discovered through him how to freely, constantly, with no fears, engage in the work of educating. The classroom work became my life. Faure opened my eyes to the importance of *thinking*, of exchanging ideas and of studying. He became my guide for many, many years.

After studying for a long time abroad I felt like a *foreigner* in my own country when I arrived back in Brazil. Intense dialogue broke down the walls. I dove into the culture and somehow, from this experience, learned to be me. This applied wherever I went in the world, and discovered "Thou" in whichever cultural situation I was to be.

My first professional friend in the U.S. was Cleo Monson. How can I forget the simplicity, the kindness, the knowledge she had of Montessori in America! Her office in the unique building facing Broadway and Fifth Avenue was a place I cherished. Later I would bring my hus-

Cleo Monson and Celma

band for a "first visit into AMS." With Cleo, I appreciated the genius of Nancy Rambusch. I enjoyed my contacts with her as they always provoked thinking.

It was at Alcuin [Montessori School], in Oak Park, that I met Dome Petrutis and Mr. and Mrs. Varnas, the pioneers of Montessori in Chicago. Trained by Maria Montessori, they knew Lubienska in 1934, the year I was born! It was through them that I grew into an understanding of what it was to be a Montessorian. They were the models of giving, thinking, and faithfully *following the child*—beyond any difficulties. I deeply admired them. Through them I was introduced to the Lithuanian culture and community.

Celma and Dome Petrutis in 1972

In Canada, working with Dome for the University of Laval, I experienced interesting moments. The best one occurred on the last day of the observation class. Dome came to me by 10:45 a.m. and asked, "Where is the snack for the children?" I quickly responded, "I will bring it at the last minute. Let's just prepare the table." She was puzzled. What was I to give to the children on the last day? Why wouldn't I tell her what I had? I remained very quiet and kept my secret. "I will bring it, do not worry." I was hiding because I had thirty cupcakes with white and pink icing left over from a party the day before—questionable nutrition, just fun! I knew that she would never give them to the children, so I hid them. When I came to the table with the cakes, all of the little children were sitting with their juice and waiting. She saw the cakes, looked at me, stood up, got her hat, and left, saying, "If you want to kill them, do it all by yourself!" I felt almost guilty. Our sixty trainee students were observing! Anyway, the children ate their cakes, survived, and happily left with their parents. Taking deep breaths for a minute to compose myself, I told the student teachers: "Follow Dome. You have a good example of how to protect the little ones." From that day on I really tried never to compromise!

The personalism of Emmanuel Mounier (1952) was very much the air I shared with all my friends in my days in Paris in 1961. His influence oriented my work, giving sense to our Montessori pedagogy. *Education indeed happens only in a personalized encounter.* We do not educate children, or students. We assist Mary, Peter, Stephen—each child individually. This passion to discover each child, each person, brought me my biggest joys in teaching.

When I take time to observe, to understand, to communicate with someone, a real I–Thou relationship happens, and I am the one who is changed by the relationship, I am the one *who becomes*.

Back in Brazil when I was fourteen years old, I was asked the names of the Great Lakes while in a geography class. I had not studied the Great Lakes. I sat for some time, and moved my eyes as though I was deep in thought. My good old teacher told me, "Never mind, Celma, you will never go there anyway." This happened in 1948.

As I arrived in Chicago in 1964, I looked at our lake like an old friend! "I made it, Lake Michigan!" And I felt so welcomed. The variety of stimuli easily available around the city of Chicago is difficult to find anywhere else.

As I have lived on various continents, I have special personal ways to express my philosophy of life and education and through this I connect with others. I still remember the first time I met Cele and Louise, two board members of the new Seton Montessori. I had a little bundle of wheat at the coffee table, as a simple decoration. Cele recognized it. She commented on it. We connected with one another, our essence, through this little sheaf of wheat.

I signed my contract at Seton in 1965, the last contract I ever signed, which gave me forever a place to be. Recognizing the other, being recognized as we are, often creates links that are the base for big enterprises. Seton and MECA were born during one of those "linking" moments. These unique encounters direct much of what happens in our lives. Many real friendships were conceived at Seton and MECA! These days I look in my heart, at each one. I celebrate each, and I am very thankful.

Friends, the Feys of dear memory, and the McLaughlins, brought me to the Chicago Symphony Orchestra and the Ravinia music festival. This introduction led to many years of regular attendance and enjoyment of the symphony.

Friends also introduced me to the University of Chicago, to Loyola, to the lake, to the suburbs. I love Chicago because of the friendships I found here. *People are the reason we love our community!*

Loyola had an outstanding professor of philosophy, Bernard Boehlen. It was in one of his classes that I first met Desmond Perry. Living alone, working intensely with little children, parents, and student teachers, made me suddenly long for a companion. Now after thirty-two years of a life together, of intense dialogue, we celebrate *the joy of being together.*

I still remember Boehlen's words:

> *All beginnings are fundamentally mysterious. Every true beginning has a creative moment for it brings something new into birth. The reality of beginning is a phenomenon of profound mysteriousness and baffles the mind, which is still open to experience and capable of wondering. The beginning of philosophy, the beginning of thinking, is wonder.* (1968, 53)

Our lives and our experiences deepen as we maintain a real dialogue and together Wonder. I owe Desmond all these years of professional life. With his quiet and reserved attitude, and intense intellectual life, he supports my work and together we are always celebrating life somewhere!

"All real living is meeting," says Martin Buber (1958, 11).

I also learned, after years of experience, that it is not necessary to look for results. As we put all our strength to discover, to see the Other, the Person whom we meet, the results just happen.

Marlene Barron, Celma, and Bretta Weiss Wolff

Paige Geiger, Celma, Aline Wolf, and Marie Dugan

All these great friendships through time and space (so many years, so many miles around the world) have made me the person you have today as a Living Legacy.

May my legacy to you be a strong call to be yourself, open to a real dialogue with the others, as it is through it that we become, that we serve. Having lived Montessori, we are to mentor others.

As Buber again says, "Only in his whole being, in all his spontaneity, can the educator truly affect the whole being of his [her] pupil…. His [her] aliveness streams out to them and affects them most strongly and purely when he [she] has no thought of affecting them" (Boehlen 1968, 254). The non-utilitarian spontaneity of authentic inspiration is the most effective and growth-provoking discipline.

Let me take a moment to thank the Board of AMS for giving me such an honor, as well as the Living Legacy committee and all those who contribute to scholarships.

Marie Dugan showed us, during just a few months as our interim executive director, *the art of giving*. Let me thank also the Illinois Montessori Society, that, in the person of Carolyn Kambich, has brought so many possibilities to our work.

My thanks to my very unique friend, Carolina Gomez del Valle, who was the first AMS Living Legacy and is not here because of her heavy obligations in Rome for the Mother House of the Ursuline Sisters.

Thanks also to my two children, Anna and Cristina; observing them mature has been, and is, one of my most rewarding and most *demanding* experiences.

To each one of you whom I met through these years of intense work: Let's celebrate our discoveries, our contacts; let's accept perhaps difficult moments. From the bottom of my heart, I thank each one of you for all you brought to my life.

And as Johnny Carson said in his last appearance, I ask you to "accept a really heartfelt thank you!"

Good night.

Let's party!

Authentic Montessori

An address at the American Montessori Society Annual Conference

Boston, MA • March 2010

By Celma Pinho Perry

We remember and honor Nancy Rambusch during this convention. She represents an important point in our lives, our personal and professional lives as Montessorians. She is at the origin of everything that we do here today. Her aim was to bring authentic Montessori to the United States. She went to Europe and even had a baby abroad. She went through a strenuous training that I know very, very well. As a result, she became a very capable educator, capable of passing her Montessori understanding on to many generations.

Going through Montessori training is like being in the desert and then emerging totally refreshed. That has been the experience of my student teachers for all these years. When they begin, they are unsure of who they are in relation to the world of education. It is as though they are in a desert and suddenly they start receiving nurturance and relating in depth. Lubienska used to say that the desert is like a materialization, a concrete way of seeing Silence—the place that is all open. It's not the absence of anything; it is openness to all.

Nancy Rambusch came here with the very definite idea of integrating Montessori within our culture, and she succeeded. She had Mario Montessori himself come to America to begin the training. Some Europeans came along—the best Montessorians available—and started the first training with her. They stayed with her until she broke relations with AMI. It was then that she started directing AMS programs in the whole of the United States. Maria Montessori passed her own wisdom to others in the beginning of the century and had done a fantastic job. At her arrival in 1913 to the United States she met Alexander Graham Bell and his wife, Mabel, and helped in starting programs. On a later trip, Maria oversaw the famous Montessori demonstration glass-walled classroom at the Panama-Pacific Exposition in San Francisco in 1915. Maria's student, Helen Parkhurst, served as the head teacher for this famous experience which lasted for four months. Many programs were started following Montessori's ideas after this display. Mrs. Parkhurst later developed the Dalton Plan, a popular Montessori-influenced schooling model on the East Coast.

In 1980, we encountered one beautifully prepared Montessori school housed in a garage in Hinsdale, IL, a suburb of Chicago. It was begun by Matilda Hiatt, who was directly trained by Maria Montessori in 1913. She ran one of the few Montessori schools in the United States that remained in operation until the 1950s. The pioneering work of Maria Montessori is carried on in the United States by Nancy McCormick Rambusch, who came with her question, "Why did Montessori education die out in the U.S.?" Her answer to me, "Because they didn't have a teacher education program!" So her main direction was, "Let's start them."

We have so many training courses today due to Nancy's preoccupation with not only promoting programs, but also assessing them. She had a very interesting book (that we used in teacher education programs) called *The Authentic American Montessori School: A Guide to the Self-Study,*

Evaluation, and Accreditation of American Schools Committed to Montessori Education (Stoops and Rambusch 1992) in which she described an authentic Montessori program and gave the tools for assessing it. She was interested in helping people analyze and continue the work as authentically as possible.

Today, when you attend an American Montessori Society teacher education program, you know that you are protected by the care and experience of the competent faculty, people that will be giving you a hand in every way, and offering constant supervision so you can give the very best that you have to your students.

Nancy also started dialogue. She lectured throughout the United States. One day on one of her visits to our program in Chicago, we were in a car with her. It was snowing, and we were able to have a long conversation. She somehow made me discover myself. She looked at me and said, "Celma! I am looking at your program. I am always very interested in the quality of information and the quality of the techniques, the Pink Tower, the Brown Stairs, and each one of these symbols of grammar—the whole program. But I am much more interested in a great strength that I see in your program. A strong program must help *initiate* the educators in the art of being. And you are doing it."

It was like a shock. I remember going inside and saying, "What am I really doing?" Today I see that one of the orientations in my life has been to deal with people in such a way that we all become more aware of ourselves. That doesn't mean perfection. That doesn't mean always being patient. That means a constant effort and a constant search for increasingly being the person I am called to be. This is why I get very close to my students: to discover who they are. I encourage them to take very good care of themselves—not only the women, but also the men. We have to be able to give our all to the children. To be able to really "do Montessori," you have to take good care of yourself because you are going to be the environment where the little children really live, whether you are working with the teenagers, or the growing children, or the administrators. The children don't learn from our teaching. They learn from our learning, as my good friend Dr. Shirley Morgenthaler often says. They assimilate through us this search for learning, their interest in the world, an interest in what exists.

Awareness of this assimilation strongly impacts the techniques of teaching, or, as I prefer, *facilitating*. Facilitating means to be there opening windows, having the child touch the world—the world outside and inside. Discover it. Celebrate. Wonder. All of this is a necessary preparation of the educator.

So, thanks to Nancy's intuition, everyone here today should be smiling. We have quality Montessori education all over the United States, and all over the world. Today Montessori is very strong and very well known.

What will make a Montessori program authentic? The basic techniques are seen in a 3–6 environment and from that we help develop at whatever level:

- In the home
- In the Infant and Toddler program
- The Early Childhood classes
- The Elementary school
- The Adolescent program
- Or even for adults:
  - Teacher education
  - Geriatric programs
  - Specific programs designed to support adults with dementia

We adapt the same basic technique for each age and need. The preschool program is the one Maria Montessori most carefully designed and worked with.

My first experience in Montessori was in France in one of the schools that Lubienska directed. I immediately observed each child working on a different activity. I observed the line being called and the children coming to it, not at the same time, but one by one as they finished their work. If all the children come immediately, she suggested that something is wrong with the way they are being called. Am I imposing?

As I came to that class, I observed the Silence Game. The children put their hands on their laps and they started to listen very quietly. I didn't know what this was. As their name was called, each one came and stayed attentively waiting. When they were all there Lubienska said, "It's a beautiful day." She had a special message that she gave them. Do we do this in our classes? At the Silence Game, we have the child there, totally open, and it is the moment to give something very special. Give a message that sends them away wondering and searching.

The Silence Game

Indeed, one of the techniques important to Authentic Montessori is the Silence Game.

I would like to give you an analysis of Lubienska's about the discovery of Silence. We need to experience it before we propose Silence Games. This is a very important Montessori technique.

> *In the beginning Silence is a discovery, like discovering a mountain, or poetry: sense of achievement in confronting a new reality before which everything that is fake disappears: joyful energy inviting the whole being to a new happy effort.* (Lubienska 1955, from the Introduction, translation mine).

As Lubienska continues,

> *We discover silence in successive levels.*

> - *At the **physical** level, while our lungs are filled with pure fresh air, our nerves tingle, our muscles are strengthened, and we feel our bodies pulsating along with the life of the universe.*

- *At the **mental** level, like at the completion of an arduous task, our thoughts master the intellectual horizon, and, seized with wonder, rest quietly.*

- *At the **spiritual** level, when, beyond reasoning and feelings, the spirit accepts and touches Life!*

Aside from those exceptional experiences where Silence takes us over, it must be conquered through effort. This is the aspect of Silence we are going to study. Intermittent at first, more habitual as we practice it, it finally becomes like the country we inhabit, a mountain, poetry. The more we stay in Silence, the more it reveals new avenues.

At whatever level it starts, Silence finds fulfillment in Life, and in a theistic approach, in God.

I will now analyze several levels of the Silence Game. *The first level is learning to be still.* It is very hard. I say at the line, "My feet are really quiet." On the first day, even the first week, perhaps, we talk almost only about the feet. "My feet are really quiet." "My hands are very quiet." "Oh, my neck is quiet." They pay attention and you can see the six-, five-, four-, and three-year-olds really tense and being able to be still. *In our lives there are two big activities—movement or no movement, and being quiet or being still.* These two totally different activities of our lives are what make us able to listen and to act. We can't educate children who are not really able to stop and be open. So the first level is learning how to be still. We do it for half a second the first time, and then a little bit more. "My feet are now going to be still for a long time. My feet rest, too. Did you tell your feet to be very quiet?"

The second level is attention. "I already know how to be still. Now I am going to be attentive—attentive to someone who calls me." So the second level is listening. Listening to the voice that calls. Listening to the voice/ sound of things. In my class I leave, perhaps, a little old faucet dripping so they hear the "drip, drip." Or I bring a clock that goes "tick tock, tick tock." I can see the child who knows how to be still, and I ask, "What can we hear in this room?" He says what he hears very spontaneously.

We want to preserve a certain natural situation, and it is interesting to have them listening to the noises from outside, too.

The third level is a new encounter at a more spiritual level. There comes a moment that normally happens by the end of the school year. Mother's Day is a very nice moment. I would bring a flower and put the flower in the center of the line. I would say to them, "Today I am thinking about my mom." They all imitate my gesture. I see them all with the same position as mine. So I wait a little bit and say, "Oh, I think my mommy's smiling." And one says, "No, she's screaming at the dog" or "She got flowers from my father" and they will all tell their different stories. It is an initiation to a meditation, to deal with someone without having the person there.

We had little music boxes and the extension of the silence went from less than a minute to over five minutes. The children really relaxed and were happy—open to life. Silence really culminates beyond meditation. It is learned from every culture. It is an encounter with life, an encounter with God. In the classroom it is an encounter with being on Earth, in the world around, even though they remain in the classroom. The little children six, seven, or eight years old are very open to it. The technique of the Silence Game is to be given daily. You have to really introduce the children to it.

There are other techniques in silence that I witnessed in several places, including Perugia with Mademoiselle Paulini. She had a beautiful class with a full balcony that went around the entire room. I was there with some students looking from the top of the balcony. Mlle. Paulini just touched a little triangle, and everyone stopped and became silent. It was so genuine and so open; she looked and she waited and waited and waited. When they were all still, she continued her work. So there are several ways of introducing the Silence Game in our lives.

We often go outside on a beautiful spring day. New flowers are there. Take the opportunity to be there, just looking and then talk about it. Avoid it being "Show and Tell." You see the little fern. You get all involved.

The children are so ready to talk about it. Tell just what is necessary. Give people space for being and for having the experience themselves.

I am not going to go into normal presentations of the material. We all know how to do it very well, and I think our teacher education programs are very strong when it comes to presentation of materials. But any time you have a discipline difficulty, anytime you have a moment of rising noise, use the Silence Game. The Silence Game is a reminder of "where am I and what am I doing?"

Another very important technique is from Miss Petrutis' class. She was a student of Maria Montessori. Miss Petrutis was teaching a classroom while I was supervising a student teacher at Ronald Knox Montessori School in Wilmette, IL. It was in October 1964. We were busy working when a little child came to her and said, "I would like to make silence." I had never heard a child request this before. Miss Petrutis said, "Oh, very good." Then the child went to the table and put his hands down. He made the silence. She was supposed to call him, but she forgot. After five minutes I started getting a little bit concerned. I looked at her and she suddenly looked at him and said, "John." He joyfully responded and then went on with his work. You have possibilities of implementing this concentration. The child is ready—able to listen—to be there. For me, this was quite an experience.

The Line

The line is also something that we do every day. If everybody comes immediately to the line, something is wrong. They will come slowly. The line is not a place for sitting down, for waiting. No way. How do you start the line? By going to the line yourself, heel-to-toe, or tiptoe, or whatever step you want. The child will follow you. Very often I start the line and nobody follows me, so after a little while I start doing something else. You are not to force the children. It has to be by invitation or by choice.

Use the best voice on the line—your own voice. Even if it is broken, it is your own singing, it is your own way of directing. No records, tapes, or

CDs are needed for having the line as a base for discipline. I do it with the children and the student teachers. I stop and everybody continues. I say, "Oh! The music stopped. Did you stop?" They had not listened to the music stopping. So I try again and again and they are barely listening. If they continue I say again, "Oh, the music stopped, I stopped." Slowly they learn to be attentive to "stop" and to follow the rhythm of what is going on. These are basic techniques without which you cannot have a Montessori class. Because they don't need to be corrected with "Don't do this!" and "Don't do that!" The line is where we all learn self-discipline and to listen.

The line is the base of discipline. It is where children learn that they can do with their feet what they want, that they can follow different rhythms. That they can stop. That they can go backward. The line is the place where they discover the relationship between their body and their mind. A teacher is never to say, "Do this, now run about." We rather say, "Would you like to run?" In Montessori, we invite. Or the teacher could say, "I like to run. I am going to run." And she will run. Some children will say "I don't feel like it right now." "That's absolutely fine. You can stay here in this room." The line is the place where you really give the children the possibility of discovering the potential they have for doing what they decide to do. "Would you tell your hands to touch your feet?" Very often I would use a sentence just like that one because I want it to empower them. They can do with their body what they want. Montessori does not correct children. So we will never say to the child, "Don't do that." *We teach teaching, not correcting.*

Anytime you have a classroom discipline difficulty or rising noise, use the Silence Game. It is a reminder of "Where am I and what am I doing?" Let's say the child puts his foot on top of a chair. Would we say to him, "Don't put your foot on the chair?" Oh no, we wouldn't say that. An authentic Montessorian would say, "Oh, I keep my feet on the floor. Such a pretty chair." Soon the child discovers that he is not supposed to put his foot on the chair. The child is a person, so we teach teaching, not correcting. Whatever we need to tell—and this is also for the home and very much for the parents—we are not there to be correcting. We are there to make the child aware of what exists and what is. That is why we use glass. That's why we use breakable things. The child that discovers will become aware—for example, he discovers glass. We do not have to say, "Be careful with glass." Let him discover by the way we touch it that it is fragile.

Grace and Courtesy

Grace and Courtesy is another important activity. The best person for this was Hilda Rothschild. Hilda was extraordinary. She was trained by Lubienska, too. My first experience with Hilda was when I was invited by Sister Jacinta to give a presentation of the Cosmos in Cincinnati. It is one of my big areas of specialty. I brought all my materials and Hilda sat down in the first row and I thought "uh oh." I didn't know her and didn't know what was going on. So I gave my whole presentation and forgot she was there. And in the end she came to me and said, "Where did you get all of my materials?" I said, "I don't know who you are; these are my materials." When we were formally introduced to one another, we learned that we had the same background from Paris, but twenty years apart. This was absolutely extraordinary! Over time, we became very, very good friends.

A very spontaneous moment occurred in Hilda's class whenever a visitor arrived. The children knew that visitors needed to be cared for. They had special visitors' materials in a corner. I told my husband when I married him that he had to see Hilda's class, so we went to Cincinnati and spent a few days observing. As he entered, a child greeted us with the question, "Do you prefer tea or coffee?" Hilda was absolutely not involved. This was in early springtime—March. In the beginning of the year she observed the children and directed them as they greeted visitors and offered refreshments, but then after the second week, she directed this activity less and less. The children became able to welcome guests because they were allowed to act on their own.

The first week we have to be very, very stable with very clear ground rules, very calm and very joyful. We have to go to bed by 9:00 p.m. in the evening instead of 10:00 because it is so draining. We have to be there, *totally present*. Once the children learn the basic setup and ground rules in this environment (they learn best if you have at least two to five children from the year before), we need to make very few changes to the environment. If we need to change a cupboard, we must wait for a vacation break or a good moment in the year, i.e., winter holidays or spring break, but, otherwise, don't make changes. Always have the work and shelves in the same place. Change the flowers, bring something new, but maintain the ground rules and the basic environment in the same way.

If we see the development of discipline as a very basic concept, Grace and Courtesy are going to be very important factors. How do we do it? We do it very gently. For instance: "How do you open a door for someone?" "How many steps are involved in opening a door? Ten or eleven!" In the beginning the child observes, and then opens the door following the observed steps. Others will come by to observe and follow. We follow the same routine with the Elementary children, on every level, and the older ones, too. "How do we introduce someone?" "How do we talk on the telephone?" "How do we wipe our lips with a napkin?"

I remember Miss Petrutis showing children how to use toilet paper in the bathroom. She showed them how to put the paper in their hand when they use the toilet. She would make a presentation of just putting the paper on their hand, so they wouldn't take the whole roll at once. How to clean their nose? How do they cough? They need Grace and Courtesy constantly. These are very important parts of discipline, and the way of relating in society.

It is not possible to be an authentic Montessorian if we are only interested in the product, or if we want to show off as a "teacher." To be an authentic Montessori teacher we must first be interested in the process. We have to be with the children, analyzing and giving techniques, and letting them do it. And we have also to be very oriented towards each child, each child's needs.

I remember in an Elementary class in Brazil I had to really look at their assignments and their work in a very specific way to help each child grow. Little Elizabeth came to me; I will never forget her. When she had done a full analysis of her book, her paper was messed up, but she had done her best and I told her, "You did the work. How do you like your work?" She went back all happy and then Sonya came. Sonya was a perfectionist. She came with a paper that was very well put together. I read it and said, "I wonder if you could have had a little bit more development. What do you mean by...?" And normally she would say, "Yes, let me think about it." This time she looked at me and said, "I just heard you talking to Elizabeth. What about me? You know, it's beautiful!" I responded, "It is beautiful, but wouldn't you like to make it even better? Go look again at Elizabeth's paper." Sonya looked at her paper, studied Elizabeth's, and then crumpled her paper. She came back later with a work of art, really the best to come from her. I will never forget either of them.

The idea of constantly analyzing the process and not focusing on showing off, on having materials work well for the others, especially with the very little ones, is extremely important. It is not the grades. It is really working for the joy of discovery. A child is a person; the techniques to develop awareness and responsibility are so important.

Be flexible. We need to avoid schedules. If a mother arrives five or ten minutes before time, do we leave them outside waiting? Isn't it possible that the child comes and helps you prepare for the day? How do you start your day in the classroom? Those are characteristics of an authentic situation. Very often playing some quiet music helps us concentrate, to be more present.

Do we have recess in our houses? A bell? Do we line up? No. We walk like people. We relate in a normal way. We do not "play school." We are in a Children's House. This respect takes away the attitude of being the boss, of being the one telling others what to do. No "recess." This word does not belong. Life has to be like a recess, or a vacation. Life has to be where we are constantly doing what is the best for us in the service of the others in our culture, in our community. Not too many rules. Basic structure, basic ground rules, but to the greatest extent possible, working like a happy family with a capable adult.

Be present. When we think about Montessori educators we have to realize the importance of being present. Did you ever talk to someone who isn't paying attention? You are talking to a person and you know that the person's mind is somewhere else. The first quality necessary to create an authentic Montessori environment is that we are present. Nothing else is important in our mind when we are with the children. The only thing important is now. It is not the time to think that we are out of milk for our own children at home. Water for one day would be lovely. It is important that we maintain our mind where our work is. We need self-discipline. When we do one thing, the other things are not important. At this moment we train ourselves. "I can do one thing at a time." We have to train ourselves as Montessori educators to be totally with one, to be totally with the task, to be present.

Be open. Another big aspect of authenticity is being open, able to receive what the child brings to us, even with the very little ones—being open to whatever they bring to us. Teaching is not giving answers. Teaching is *questioning together.* "Where is the glue?" How do you answer? "Oh let's see, where could the glue be?" We are not saying, "It is right there. Don't you remember?" We share the question, "Where is the glue?" We don't say, "I am not going to tell you, you are supposed to know!" We teach teaching, not correcting, with an attitude in which the child can freely discover. If we see that they come to us too often to show and to ask our ideas, something is wrong with our way of directing. We have to direct in such a way that the child is totally independent from us. If children are waiting for our direction, asking "What do I do now?" something is wrong with the way we direct.

Maria Montessori was very strong in saying that you do not accept what is wrong, that you do not accept the evil. But you do it in a very simple and direct way. Say a child tells me, "Johnny is hurting me." If the situation is normal, I'd say, "Did he hurt you?" "Then go and tell him, don't hurt me! I would go and tell him, 'Don't touch me. Don't hurt me.'" I remember seeing this little boy after this conversation going to the other big child and saying, "You don't touch me again!" *We empower the child.* We do not solve their problems. We empower them to solve problems. Any time we solve their problems, we are diminishing the child.

To be an educator we have to be present, to be open, to be questioning with the children; we must give them time and respect their rhythm. We need to control and assess ourselves. Why do I have so many children coming to me? Why aren't Johnny or Peter doing more on their own?

When we talk about a *child as a person*, the two correct tendencies of a human being, of a human life, are the *capacity of thinking* and the *capacity of choosing*.

Awareness of reality. In summary I say: to educate is to be with the other in such a way that the other becomes aware of reality. The child as a person is someone that needs to be aware—aware of who he is, how he feels. "It seems to me that you are very upset?" Our main responsibility as educators is to make each child aware, aware of himself first, aware of his power. "It looks like you really can draw. It looks like you really love yellow." We can help each one discover their own being, making them more and more aware of themselves, and aware of the others. "It looks like Johnny doesn't like it when you take his pencil, does he?"

This is awareness of what exists. We have to communicate with the child, because it is from our learning that he is going to learn, from our discovering that he is going to discover the world. The attitude of an educator that knows the child's ability can help the child become aware. It's not telling him things. It's finding a way for him to discover the same awareness at home: "Mother, I need my hat. Where is my hat?" What would a mother normally say? "I put it in the cupboard like I always do." The child will feel guilty because he has forgotten where he put the hat. When the child asks, "Where is my hat?" we should answer, "Oh, where is your hat? I would help you find it, but I am so busy. Look around. Perhaps it is in the kitchen." So he finds it himself and feels freed. This has to become a habit, something we do all the time.

Children are discovering reality. Especially when they are very young they are discovering the reality of self, reality of the other, reality of the world around them. You may have heard the story about the cream. A mother asked a father, "Would you go across the park and get me a pint of cream? I have guests and I forgot the cream." The father responded, "For sure." So the father called his little three-year-old daughter and they went through the park to the market to buy the cream. The father's intention was to buy the cream, but the need of the child was to discover the park. So she found a yellow leaf with a drop of water, and then a little insect, and her dad said, "Come on! Come on!" The aim of the adult was only to do the task. The aim of the child was to discover the world.

Children are constantly attentive. When I went to my daughter's house to visit, I didn't know what to do to turn on the television for a program. Her four-year-old son said, "You just press this little button." I wondered, how he knew this when he never watched TV? He must have seen it once or twice, Mother and Daddy doing it, and he is aware of what to do.

We need to introduce new items each day so that coming to school is always an experience. I remember when the first men went to the moon in 1969. I couldn't go to sleep. I spent the next day watching television and reading magazines. I cut pictures and made cards from the newspaper for the classroom. I had to introduce my students to the life of the world. I needed to research more and more for myself. That's why teaching makes us better people, because we are constantly looking for more, so we can research and we can be present. This awareness is very, very important; our main task is to help the child be aware.

It is important not to interfere when a child is doing something. Let's say the child is writing on a paper and you come and just gently align the paper in another direction. No, don't do it. We disturb his work. *Unnecessary interference disrupts development.* We really need to be firm about that. We need to respect the concentration of the child who is working, who is involved. We don't touch them or their work. Let's imagine that child just finished a material but left it on the rug and walked away. He went somewhere else where he found another work and started. We do not interfere at the moment he discovered something else and say, "Look, you forgot your material over there. Come on." No. We wait patiently until we see that his interest is low, then, we say, "Can I help you put the work away that you forgot?" And if he says, "I don't want to," what do you say? "Oh, okay, I can do it. You must be tired. I am all right. I will help you. We can work together."

I was visiting a parent and they had this beautiful place for the children to work very close to the kitchen so the mother could cook. She told me, "I don't know what you put in the juice at school, because this place here is a mess all the time, they never put things back as they do with you." I asked her, "Do you like to put things away?" From that day she started enjoying putting things away, and so did her children. At school, the children see one another complete activities. One is going to do what the others do, because it is fun.

What helps in the community is an attitude of celebration, of being to-gether and accepting one another. Take care of your assistants, take care of the ones that are close to your children. Give them a good life. I had a student teacher who would disappear from the classroom every day at 10:00 a.m., just at the moment when the children became a little bit noisy. So one day I asked her, "Could you prepare the pencils the day before instead of at 10:00 a.m.?" She looked at me and said, "Celma, if I don't leave, I will collapse. At 10:00 a.m. I can't stand anymore." Let's know who our people are. Let's serve them. Let's celebrate with them. When do we call the children for the "line" and when is it best to do the Silence Game? We need to make very sure that our assistant is ready to help others, so we can really concentrate and be with the children enjoying the line or the Silence.

Authentic Montessori programs develop Awareness and Responsibility in the child.

☙

Authentic Montessori, Chicago Style

An address to the American Montessori Society Annual Conference

Chicago, IL • March 2011

by Celma Pinho Perry

From 1959, when Dr. and Mrs. Dunn met Nancy Rambusch, to the present day, Montessori in Chicago has had a long history of excellence. This workshop will offer an analysis of how the Montessori approach has been adapted to the American culture here, illuminating essential patterns of acculturation for Montessori schools everywhere. Among the many topics to be addressed are starting a Children's House, essential techniques of Authentic Montessori, and the influence of AMS founder Dr. Nancy McCormick Rambusch's message of cultural adaptation.

Timeline of Montessori from
Casa dei Bambini, Rome, 1907, to America, to Chicago

PART A: Montessori Visits America

1907   Opening of Casa dei Bambini, San Lorenzo, Rome
When choosing an assistant, Montessori decided on
someone who truly cared about and was interested in
children

1909   First report of Montessori education in America—an
article written in *The Kindergarten Primary Magazine* at
the National Louis College in Evanston, IL. Kings and
professors begin observing and admiring in awe. "How
can these children act like this? What is going on?"

1910   Montessori school opened by Matilda Hiatt in Hinsdale,
IL, a suburb of Chicago: this one-room schoolhouse
closed in 1953

1911   First Montessori schools open in Tarrytown, NY, Boston,
MA, and the North Side of Chicago (joining Hinsdale in
the Midwest)

1912   Harvard University publishes the English translation of
The Montessori Method

1913   First presentation of the Montessori Method in
English-spoken (translated) courses, Rome, Italy.

1913   First visit of Maria Montessori to America

1915   The Glass Classroom—Panama Pacific International Exposition in San Francisco. This demonstration class was
such an important opportunity for teachers and parents
to follow the child.

            Maria Montessori runs the Los Angeles Montessori
Training Course

| 1915 | Beginning of many Children's Houses in the United States, including a Montessori school in Winnetka, a northern suburb of Chicago |

PART B: Nancy Rambusch and the Founding of the AMS

1950	Nancy McCormick Rambusch "happens" upon *The Montessori Method* in French. She contacts Mario Montessori, who tells her the best training course was in London, so off to London she goes.
1954	Rambusch takes the Montessori teacher training course in England and comes back to the States immediately afterward
1955	Rambusch starts a "Montessori-type" playgroup in her home; she had two small children of her own by that time. She was very involved with the Catholic movement.
1956	She moves to Greenwich, CT, and lectures extensively around the country
1958	She starts the Whitby school in Connecticut, which is in operation today
1959	She starts teacher training classes
1960	She founds the American Montessori Society; reflects on interrelationships between culture and development; and promotes start of American teacher education courses in the United States with the philosophical input of John McDermott

PART C: Montessori in the Chicago area

1910–1953	Matilda Hiatt operates a Montessori program in Hinsdale, IL
1913	First visit of Maria Montessori to Chicago
1913	Elizabeth Harrison from National Louis University in Chicago brings Montessori influences to her "innovative mothers and teachers classes." These classes give parents basic ideas of parenting using many of Froebel's ideas.

The Montessori movement, which was expanding in 1913, begins slowing as the different American Montessori experiments die with their founders.

1958	The Lithuanian Montessori Society is organized in Chicago
1958	Kathy and Paul Dunn, interested in children's education, go to Notre Dame University for a meeting of Christian Family Movement. They meet John Grady and subscribe to *Jubilee* magazine (Nancy Rambusch's husband was the magazine's art editor). Through this, they hear about the Montessori Method.
1959	Kathy Dunn goes to Greenwich to meet Nancy Rambusch, who gives her names of two future teachers, John Grady and wife Therese

At a New Year's party at the Dunns' house, Francis and Fran Roach and William and Marjorie Buckingham pledge to start a Montessori school in Oak Park, IL

Nine more couples join in, and created The Montessori Society of Chicago (among them was Urban Fleege)

1959–

1963　　　Maria Varnas and Dome Petrutis run Zidinelis, a Montessori Children's House, in their own home because they wanted Montessori schooling for the Lithuanian children from their community (and the three of them had done the same in Lithuania before they came to the United States).

1961　　　Nancy Rambusch visits Chicago and lectures at The Lithuanian Montessori Society (directed by Mrs. Vaisvila), and at DePaul University (where Urban Fleege was vice president)

Alcuin Montessori opens in Oak Park, IL; Mrs. Varnas and Miss Petrutis become advisors

1962　　　Ancona School opens on the South Side of Chicago

1963　　　Montessori schools open throughout the state:

- Ronald Knox Montessori School Wilmette Il

- Cabrini Green (a Head Start program) in downtown Chicago, led by Marcella Morrison

- Lithuanian Children's Houses on the South Side of Chicago, led by Stase Vaisvila

- Beverly Montessori (Champaign-Urbana), led by Irene Kenneth Voros

1963　　　AMS Convention is held at the Edgewater Beach Hotel, Chicago, led by Cleo Monson, secretary of AMS, and facilitated by Urban Fleege.

1964　　　Alcuin teacher training program is started by Urban Fleege (teacher trainers were Dome Petrutis, Hilda Rothschild (also trained by Lubienska), Maria Varnas, Lena Wickramaratne, Katherine Kenneth, Ann Murphy. The first course has 37 students. In August 1964, Celma Pinho joins the core group.

1964	Celma Pinho, student of Lubienska de Lenval and Pierre Faure, arrives at Alcuin and becomes a supervisor of the teacher training program.
1965	Seton Montessori School is started by a group of parents, and is designed and coordinated by Celma Pinho
1965	Midwest Montessori Teacher Training Center is started by Urban Fleege
1966	A second Alcuin teacher training program is started, directed by Celma Pinho and Dome Petrutis
1970	MECA-Seton teacher education program is started, directed by Celma Pinho, with a strong emphasis on prenatal parenting (family awareness of the importance of the nine months' gestation in the full development of a human life) and early parenting. Lectures are given in high schools and at parent open houses.
1974	Celma and Desmond Perry, along with baby Anna, eight months old, give a lecture and live demonstration of the Montessori infant floor bed at the NAEYC Conference in Washington, D.C.

PART D: Montessori, Chicago's Own

As I travel around the world visiting student teachers and Montessori Children's Houses, I recognize again and again Dome Petrutis's relevance as a teacher educator and her long-lasting legacy. Chicago was the birthplace of several Montessori concepts that continue today.

1. The washing hands activity techniques, using a handwashing stand, are unique to Chicago, as the stand was created there by Mr. Varnas in the early 1960s for use in the Montessori school in his home. It is a Practical Life experience that is far more than handwashing: it cultivates attention and the discovery of the hands, and brings peace and relaxation. Many of us now use a specially built hand-washing stand in our Mon-

tessori classrooms, and this has become widespread, from its start in Chicago to many other parts of the country and the world!

- The stand is set with two towels, one for drying the hands, the other for drying the bowl

- A small bar of soap, soap dish, a pretty bowl (always glass or ceramic, never plastic), and a pitcher and bucket

- The stand always faces the area where children work to call the child to observe the classroom

- It is used many times during the day in a Montessori classroom

We observe that younger children do washing activities only if their hands or dishes are clean; they do it for the pleasure of washing, a full experience of who they are—a normalization. Each finger is washed and dried. After the age of four and a half they wash only when the dishes or their hands are dirty.

2. The Sandpaper Letters were designed by Professor Varnas and introduced in the teacher education classes by Dome Petrutis.

- We have two sets, one for right-handed children and another for left-handed children, with the letter pasted on the right or left accordingly.

- Vowels are pink, consonants are blue.

- Letters match precisely so words can be formed—this is an example of isolation of difficulty.

- Sandpaper Letters have three parts: the body of the letter in the center of each card, and then the upper section and the lower section (each as needed). All the cards should be sized to include all three parts. This way all the cards are the same size and can be lined up evenly to make words.

3. The presentation and the development of the use of Metal Insets has a unique emphasis and comes from the Lithuanian influence in Chicago.

- Each child has a box for his own collection of Metal Insets.

- He chooses a pencil holder, and chooses the colors from the Prismacolor collection. Quality materials are important, including a pencil that really works

- He chooses a #2 pencil for outlining the Inset's shape

- He chooses a piece of cardboard that is a centimeter wider than the Metal Inset paper around all its edges

- He chooses a piece of paper to be centered on the cardboard, which is prepared with one centimeter of border around the size of the paper.

The result of all this special presentation is an evolution from very simple tentative outlining of the Metal Inset forms to beautiful designs that children create on their own and are proud of. Meanwhile, they are preparing their hands for writing and developing artistic sensibilities!

4. The line (Chicago-style): a well-designed line affixed to the floor, often with tape, sometimes painted, used for refining movement and body awareness.

Here the child is becoming aware of his/her body. It is a way of becoming aware of how I move, the rhythm, how I stop, etc. Lubienska recognized that the line offers a way of developing discipline (e.g., we listen to the music, we follow a rhythm, we become aware of our body). These activities were inspired by Montessori, influenced by Lubienska, and refined by early Chicago Montessorians.

5. The low bed for infants and toddlers in the Montessori community: This concept was introduced in 1973, mostly by Celma and Desmond Perry, and was popularized in Chicago, and reproduced all around the world by our students and other Montessorians who have taken this idea to heart. It is different than just putting a mattress on the floor. The bed must be as close to the ground as possible so the child is free to move, while allowing for airflow under the bed. The floor bed allows the mobile child to be independent — there are no bars or cage. In addition, the bedroom must be a safe space for the child to move independently and freely.

Montessori is very simple, very human, very demanding. It asks us to be aware of ourselves, responsible in every way. The way I look and the way I move are being observed by the children. We

Cristina and Anna as toddlers, demonstrating the Montessori floor bed.

must be there totally for the children. We must maintain their interest, facilitating them, opening the Cosmos to them.

Author note: information for this address came from the following independently shared unpublished papers:

Griffin, M.J., *"The Early Years of Alcuin Montessori"*

Maciulis, V., *"Beginnings in Illinois"*

❧

THE DISCOVERY OF SILENCE

Excerpted, translated, and adapted
by Celma Pinho Perry, most recently in 2012

By Hélène Lubienska de Lenval

This section from the book *Le Silence: À l'Ombre de la Parole,* by Hélène Lubienska de Lenval (1955, from the Introduction), has been foundational in my work and I have given it to countless student teachers over the years as they begin their Montessori preparation.

***

In the beginning Silence is a discovery, like discovering a mountain, or poetry: sense of achievement in confronting a new reality before which everything that is fake disappears: joyful energy inviting the whole being to a new happy effort.

We discover Silence in successive levels.

At the **physical level***, while our lungs are filled with pure fresh air, our nerves tingle, our muscles are strengthened, we feel our bodies pulsating along with the life of the universe.*

*At the **mental level**, like at the completion of an arduous task, our thoughts master the intellectual horizon and, seized with wonder, rest quietly.*

*At the **spiritual level**, when, beyond reasoning and feelings, the spirit accepts and touches Life!*

Aside from those exceptional experiences where Silence takes us over, it must be conquered through effort. This is the aspect of silence we are going to study. Intermittent at first, more habitual as we practice it, it finally becomes like the country we inhabit, a mountain, poetry. The more we stay in Silence the more it reveals new avenues.

At whatever level it starts, Silence finds fulfillment in Life, in a theistic approach, in God.

REFERENCES

Aquinas, Thomas. year unknown. *De Magistro ("On the Teacher")*. Accessed October 2015. http://www4.desales.edu/~philtheo/loughlin/ATP/De_Magistro/De_Magistro_11_1.html

Boehlen, Bernard J. 1968. *Existential Thinking*. Pittsburgh, PA: Duquesne University Press.

Bruner, Jerome. 1977. *The Process of Education*. Cambridge, MA: Harvard University Press.

Buber, Martin. 1958. *I and Thou*. New York: Charles Scribner's Sons.

Csikszentmihalyi, Mihaly. 1990. *Flow: The Psychology of Optimal Experience*. New York: Harper & Row.

de Saint-Exupery, Antoine. 1943. *The Little Prince*. New York: Harcourt Brace.

Erikson, Erik. 1974. *Dimensions of a New Identity: The 1973 Jefferson Lectures in the Humanities*. New York, NY: W. W. Norton & Co. Inc.

Freire, Paulo. 1970. *Pedagogy of the Oppressed*. New York: Herder and Herder.

Gopnik, Alison, Andrew N. Meltzoff, and Patricia K. Kuhl (1999). *The Scientist in the Crib: What Early Learning Tells Us About the Mind*. New York: William Morrow.

Hechinger, Fred M., ed. 1966. *Pre-School Education Today*. New York: Doubleday.

Itard, Jean-Marc-Gaspard. 1962. *The Wild Boy of Aveyron*. Translated by George and Muriel Humphrey. New York: Prentice-Hall.

Kahn, David. 1997. "Foreword: Finding Flow in Montessori." *The NAMTA Journal*, v22, n2.

Kamii, Constance and Rheta DeVries. 1976. *Piaget, Children, and Number: Applying Piaget's Theory to the Teaching of Elementary Number*. Washington, DC: NAEYC.

Liegé, A. 1958. *Adultes dans le Christ*. Belgium: La Pensee Catholique.

Lubienska de Lenval, Hélène. 1950. *A Educação do Homem Consciente: Desenvolvimento Físico, Psíquico E Espiritual*. Translated and adapted to Portuguese by Celma Pinho (Sister Maria Ana). São Paulo, Brazil: Flamboyant.

1950. *L'Education de L'Homme Conscient*. Paris: Spes.

1957. *Le Silence: À l'Ombre de la Parole*. Paris: Casterman Tournay.

Maslow, Abraham H. 1962. *Toward A Psychology of Being*. New York: Van Nostrand Company, Inc.

McLuhan, Marshall. 1964. *Understanding Media: The Extension of Man*. New York: Mentor.

Montessori, Maria. 1963. *The Absorbent Mind*. Adyar, India: The Theological Publishing House.

1956. *The Child in the Family*. New York: Avon Books.

1967. *The Discovery of the Child*. Notre Dame, IN: Fides Publishers, Inc.

1949/1989. *The Formation of Man*. Santa Barbara, CA: ABC-Clio LTD. Accessed October 2015. http://www.montessoriteacherscollective.com/abcclio/basic.html

1912. *The Montessori Method*. New York: Frederick A. Stokes Company.

1936. *The Secret of Childhood*. Calcutta, India: Orient Longman.

1981. *The Secret of Childhood*. New York, NY: Ballantine Books.

Morgenthaler, Shirley. Lecture presented at the Chicago Metro Association for Young Children's Annual Conference; Chicago, IL, January 1992.

Mounier, Emmanuel. 1952. *Personalism*. London: Routledge and Paul.

NAEYC. July 2009. "NAEYC Standards for Early Childhood Professional Preparation Programs." Accessed October 2015. https://www.naeyc.org/files/naeyc/file/positions/ProfPrepStandards09.pdf

Orem, R.C., ed.1967. *Montessori for the Disadvantaged: An Application of Montessori's Educational Principles to the War on Poverty*. New York: Putnam.

Perry, Celma. 1980. "Revitalizing the Montessori Apparatus." *The Constructive Triangle*, v7, n3: 7–13.

Perry, Celma Pinho and Seton staff. 1981. "A Montessori All-Day Program." *The Constructive Triangle*, v8, n4: 16–20.

Perry, Celma. 1986. *Facilitating a Montessori All Day Program*. Chicago: Seton Montessori Institute Publications (previously MECA-Seton).

Perry, Desmond. 1974. *The Child Is a Person*. Chicago: Seton Montessori Institute Publications (previously MECA-Seton).

1975, 2010. Perceptual Motor Development. Chicago: Seton Montessori Institute Publications (previously MECA-Seton).

Piaget, Jean and Barbel Inhelder. 1969. *The Psychology of the Child*. Translated by Helen Weaver. New York: Basic Books.

Rambusch, Nancy McCormick. 2013. *Learning How to Learn: An American Approach to Montessori*. Santa Rosa, CA: Parent Child Press, a division of Montessori Services.

Rambusch, Nancy McCormick and John A. Stoops. 1992. *The Authentic American Montessori School: A Guide to the Self-Study, Evaluation, and Accreditation of American Schools Committed to Montessori Education.* New York: American Montessori Society and The Commission on Elementary Schools of The Middle States Association.

Rogers, Carl. 1961. *On Becoming A Person: A Therapist's View of Psychotherapy.* Boston: Houghton Mifflin.

Schön, Donald A. 1987. *Educating the Reflective Practitioner.* New York: Basic Books.

Tabors, Patton O. 1997. *One Child, Two Languages: A Guide for Early Childhood Educators of Children Learning English as a Second Language.* Baltimore, MD: Brookes Publishing.

Williams, Margery. 1946. *The Velveteen Rabbit.* New York: Doubleday.

Independently Shared Unpublished Papers (used for "Authentic Montessori, Chicago Style," page 117):

Griffin, M.J., *"The Early Years of Alcuin Montessori"*

Maciulis, V., *"Beginnings in Illinois"*

೧೪

SUGGESTED READING

Bruner, Jerome. 1971. *The Relevance of Education*. New York: Norton & Company.

Chattin-McNichols, John. 1992. *The Montessori Controversy*. Albany, NY: Delmar.

Elkind, David. 1970. *Children and Adolescence (Interpretative Essays on Jean Piaget)*. New York: Oxford University Press.

Faure, Pierre. 1957. *Au Siècle de l'Enfant*. Paris: Mame.

Faure, Pierre. 1979. *Un Enseignement Personnalisé et Communautaire*. Paris: Casterman.

Hainstock, Elizabeth G. 1971. *Teaching Montessori in the Home*. New York: Random House.

Illich, Ivan. 1971. *Deschooling Society*. New York: Harper and Row.

Kamii, Constance. 1973. "Piaget's Interactionism and the Process of Teaching Young Children" in *Piaget in the Classroom*, edited by Milton Schwebel and Jane Raph. New York: Basic Books.

Loeffler, Margaret Howard. 1992. *Montessori in Contemporary American Culture*. New York: Heinemann.

Lubienska de Lenval, Hélène. 1953. *Entrainement a L'Attention*. Paris: Spes.

1962. *La Methode Montessori*. Paris: Spes.

1957–1961. *The Whole Man at Worship*. Paris: Desclée.

Montanaro, Silvana Quattrocchi, M.D. 1987. *Understanding the Human Being: The Importance of the First Three Years of Life*. Mountain View, CA: Neinhuis.

Montessori, Maria. 1956. *Dr. Montessori's Own Handbook*. New York: Schocken Books.

Montessori, Maria. 1948. *To Educate the Human Potential*. Madras, India: Kalakshetra.

Perry, Desmond. 2001. *The Child: What Every Caring Parent Needs to Know*. Chicago: Seton Montessori Institute Publications (previously MECA-Seton).

Perry, Desmond and Seton Faculty. 1983. *The Toddler Program*. Reviewed and updated by Carolina Gomez del Valle. Chicago: Seton Montessori Institute Publications (previously MECA-Seton).

Pinho, Celma. 1969. *A Montessori Curriculum 3 to 6* (brochure). New York: American Montessori Society.

Perry, Celma. 1970. *The Cosmic Approach*. Chicago: Seton Montessori Institute Publications (previously MECA-Seton).

Piaget, Jean. 1966. *The Origins of Intelligence in Children*. Translated by Margaret Cook. New York: International Universities Press.

Povell, Phyllis. 2010. *Montessori Comes to America: The Leadership of Maria Montessori and Nancy McCormick Rambusch*. Lanham, MD: University Press of America.

Ribble, Margaret. 1965. *Rights of Infants*, 2nd ed. New York: Columbia University.

Rogers, Carl. 1969. *Freedom to Learn*. Columbus, OH: Charles E. Merrill Publishers.

Salk, Lee and Rita Kramer. 1973. *How To Raise a Human Being: A Parent's Guide to Emotional Health from Infancy Through Adolescence*. New York: Warner.

Wolf, Aline D. 2014. *Nurturing the Spirit in Non-Sectarian Classrooms*. Santa Rosa, CA: Parent Child Press, a division of Montessori Services.

❧

ACKNOWLEDGMENTS

This book reflects my thoughts, my life, and my professional orientation during my fifty-plus years of work in the United States.

I arrived in Chicago in 1964, a few years after the creation of the American Montessori Society (AMS). I am deeply thankful for the trust given to me throughout all these years of work with the Society.

The American Montessori Society had just recently been founded. Meeting Cleo Monson was the first step in a long relationship. I shared AMS's aims and worked relentlessly to create authentic Montessori Children's Houses in the United States. Soon I discovered that Nancy McCormick Rambusch had the same European Montessori background that I had. I became aware of how much life she brought to the Montessori movement. Her stamina and passion were contagious!

To all my student teachers, to all the parents in our schools, to all the children I welcomed in my classes, thank you! Knowing you has helped me become more and more the person I was called to be.

Desmond Perry, my very capable husband and lifelong partner, with my two children, Anna and Cristina, created an environment at home where I felt secure and happy. Cristina's artistic sensibility continues to inspire me each day.

My appreciation in the publishing of these notes goes first to Lynn Sellers, my secretary for over twenty-five years who typed all my lectures to distribute to our student teachers. My deepest thanks for the initial reviewing job made by my remarkable former student, and now colleague for years, Drina Madden, for her understanding of my Montessori philosophy and her skill to translate into correct American English my many papers written between 1964 and 2014.

To my trusted friends and colleagues who read, corrected, and encouraged the publication of these papers, and especially for the expertise of Robert Simerly in editing my personal story, I offer my deep gratitude!

Our deep appreciation goes to Montessori Services and all those involved at Parent Child Press. Jane Campbell's precision, and her choice of Carey Jones as developmental editor, made this book a reality. I also express my thanks to each of the photographers who allowed their beautiful work to be included in this publication: Moira Nolan Photography, Matt Jones Photography, Giovanni Photography, Sonia Mani-Joseph Photography, Petra Singerhoff, and Don Parrucci.

But it is my daughter, Anna Perry, who has been my most intimate professional friend and who carries the responsibility of continuing Seton's tradition (including supporting the publication of this volume), whom I wholeheartedly thank!

Obrigada, merci, gracias,
thank you!

Seton Montessori School: A Children's House
5728 Virginia Street, Clarendon Hills, IL 60514

138

"Celma Perry began her story as a contemplative and a revolutionary and she continues to be so: her writings celebrate being fully involved in reality, questioning together with the child, demonstrating total presence and attention, and understanding silence. Celma gives us the way to become, as Maria Montessori recommends, 'a scientist and a saint.'"

~ *Carolina Gomez del Valle, OSU*
First recipient of the AMS Living Legacy Award

"Celma's lectures are based on a profound understanding of Maria Montessori's work: the child's stages of development, psychological needs, and spiritual power. I applaud the revival of these lectures for educators and parents to better understand the child and to work for a better world."

~ *Marcia Tavares de Lima*
Founder of Prima Escola Montessori, Sao Paulo, Brazil

To hear some of Celma's most popular lectures
from AMS conferences of the past, please visit:

http://setonmontessori.org/institute/celmaperry/